To: Marta

From: Sheryl

Date: 21 NOV 2014

To your Success!

Sheryl L. Roush

Heart

of a Woman *in* Business

Stories, strategies and
skills for business success

Sheryl L. Roush

SPARKLE PRESS
SAN DIEGO, CALIFORNIA

Published by Sparkle Press
A division of Sparkle Presentations, Inc.
Post Office Box 2373, La Mesa, California 91943 USA

Send contributions to Sheryl@HeartBookSeries.com
Visit our website at: www.HeartBookSeries.com

Second Printing March 2010
Library of Congress Control Number: 2008908009

Library of Congress Cataloging-in-Publication Data
Roush, Sheryl Lynn.
Heart of a Woman in Business
Stories, strategies and skills for business success/Sheryl L. Roush
ISBN 10: 1-880878-20-8
ISBN 13: 978-1-880878-19-4

1. Self-Help 2. Inspirational 3. Women's Issues

Printed in the United States of America.

Contents

Fulfilling Your Soul / 37

Polishing Up on Business Skills / 61

Committing to Excellence / 91

Light Moments / 111

Best Practices, Strategies & Ideas / 119

Businesswomen & Motherhood / 153

From a Day Job to My Own Job / 167

Entrepreneurial Spirit / 183

Business Builders / 209

Nurturing Our Mind, Body, & Spirit / 225

Whispers of Wisdom / 249

Uplifting the Spirit / 259

◆ ◆ ◆

Author Information / 269

Introduction

*T*his collection is dedicated to women in the workplace—be it at a job in our chosen field or one we found along our career path. Employed or self-employed. "Sisters" share their tips, ideas, and insights for raising the bar, striving for success and living dreams.

We bring balance to chaotic environments, inspiring cooperation and harmony. We bring our gifts of vision, intuition, and creativity to whatever we do—and wherever we choose to do it. Our jobs do not define us. Instead, we bring our essence to our jobs—in our choice of service to others and the world. How we serve others is an extension of our love as we joyfully align with our gifts and our authenticity. More than ever before our voices are heard and our skills are respected.

I determined at thirteen that life is too short to have a job I don't like. If I couldn't find a job to do what I wanted to do, I would create my own . . . and at sixteen started my first of eight businesses. I held executive positions and succeeded in positions that were stereotypically held by men. These jobs were vital training for what I do today, helping organizations create positive work environments, boost motivation, and improve morale.

Many of my contributing co-authors have similar stories. The core message of this book is about having that passion—every day— for what we do. May you celebrate these inspirations for your spirit, skills for your mind, and nurturing for your body, and may you find *your* success.

From my heart to yours,

Sheryl

HEART OF A WOMAN IN BUSINESS

A woman in business is like no other
Multi-brilliant at work, and often too, a mother.

Guided by vision to make a difference in this world,
Reporting for service, with her hair even curled.

Ready to go, whenever the need
She knows in her heart, there's a calling to feed.

To do right, to speak up, determined to succeed
A role model that plants the possibility seed.

Knows who she is, right down to the core
Her essence, her passion—shine all the more!

She's in charge with a handle on it all.
At the office, at home, or at the mall.

Even in the depth of all she may know
Realizes there's still plenty room to grow.

So energetic, creative and fun . . .
Early rise, there's much to be done!

She still finds time to laugh and to play
Sacred time too, to kneel and to pray

It comes from inside, driven by vision,
Get on board—she's on a great mission!

Her daily prayer resides in God's grace
Serving others from her heart sets the pace

Making use of her talent, wisdom and skill
From strengths and trust in Divine will.

Gentle, compassionate, loving and strong
In this sisterhood of success you want to belong

Anything she puts her heart to she can do
She's not alone sis'ta—as you can too!

The road to get here has been quite a ride
"Call me 'Woman'— it's my source of pride!"

Come along, she's blazin' new trail
A woman in business—whom we all hail!

~ SHERYL ROUSH
Speaker, Sparkle Presentations, Inc.
© 2008 Sheryl L. Roush

Inspirations for the Heart

Fulfill Your Heart's Desire

*H*ave you ever had one of those moments—when life forces you to take a close look inside your heart and soul? Yes, this is when you begin to discover your true answers.

What answers do you hear when you listen to your heart? I can tell you they are not answers rooted in fear, doubt, worry or lack. They are answers anchored in love, possibility, hope, faith, belief and authentic desire.

Don't wait until you "know it all" before you start to fulfill your heart's desire, because chances are, you'll never know enough. Get started on your dreams; trust the universe to show you and teach you what you need to be successful. When you truly listen and follow your heart and have a clear vision of how you'll serve others, the universe comes to help you in miraculous ways.

Trust your heart. Ask for its input and how it feels about a decision and then let it guide you. Whatever you dream of is yours for the asking. This is not to say it will be handed to you on a silver platter. But it will be given to you if you maintain faith and continue to be guided by your true desire.

Your heart is your compass; let it point you in the direction of your dreams.

~ CHRISTINE KLOSER
Speaker, Author, Founder of Network for Empowering Women
© 2004 Christine Kloser, Excerpt from Inspiration to Realization: Real Women Reveal Proven Strategies for Personal, Business, Financial and Spiritual Fulfillment

WHO AM I TO BE BRILLIANT?

Our deepest fear is not that we are inadequate. Our deepest fear is that we are powerful beyond measure. It is our light, not our darkness that frightens us most. We ask ourselves, "Who am I to be brilliant, gorgeous, talented, and famous?" Actually, who are you not to be? You are a child of God. Your playing small does not serve the world. There is nothing enlightened about shrinking so that people won't feel insecure around you. We were born to make manifest the glory of God that is within us. It's not just in some of us; it's in all of us. And when we let our own light shine, we unconsciously give other people permission to do the same. As we are liberated from our own fear, our presence automatically liberates others.

~ MARIANNE WILLIAMSON
From A Return to Love

❖ ❖ ❖

A bird doesn't sing because it has an answer, it sings because it has a song.
~ MAYA ANGELOU

Until you live your life for something bigger than yourself your world will always remain very small.

~ J.F. SCOTT

Success to me is not about money or status or fame, it's about finding a livelihood that brings me joy and self-sufficiency and a sense of contributing to the world.

~ ANITA RODDICK
Founder of The Body Shop

THE LAW OF ACTION

*A*ctions speak louder than words. Action is the most important success habit anyone possesses when it comes to determining how your business and personal life play out. Ideas, knowledge, and expertise are all useless without action, because action is the starting point of all progress.

Successful people are those who recognize an opportunity and then take quick action. You too can learn how to do this, by developing a powerful business skill that will transform your life forever—the skill of taking action.

The good news is that you don't have to wait until you know more, do more or achieve more to take action. If you wait until conditions are perfect, you'll be waiting forever. The best time to take action is right now.

I have actually achieved most of my business success from taking action on things I knew nothing about. In fact, I've never applied for a job in my life, never attended a day of college, and started every one of my businesses with little or no knowledge of the industry I was going into. Now, I am not recommending that you do the same. But I do recommend that you take action when opportunities arise instead of sitting back and waiting for the timing to be just right. Often opportunities for success knock on your door before you think you are ready. That's all right. Open the door and step out anyway!

You're going to make some mistakes along the way, but taking action will move you forward faster than standing still. Even if you take two steps forward and one step back you're getting ahead. With each step you will become more knowledgeable, confident, and successful.

Are you ready to move forward and manifest the success you desire today? One of the best steps to taking action is to become a doer. Actually practice doing more of the things you are currently just thinking or dreaming about. What is it you really want to do?

- *Do you want to start a new business?*
- *Do you want to lose weight or get in better shape?*
- *Do you want to become more successful in business or the career you currently possess?*
- *Do you want to excel and achieve more sales goals this year?*

Whatever it is, start doing it—*today*!

The longer an idea, concept, or dream rattles around in your head without action, the weaker it becomes. After a while you lose clarity and you begin to forget about your ideas. Ideas are important, but they will only benefit you when you implement them. One simple idea put into action is more valuable than dozens of brilliant ideas that are saved until the perfect opportunity arises. Unless you take action, those ideas will never go anywhere. Action truly speaks louder than words!

Doers accomplish more and stimulate even more ideas in the process. That means they can take more positive action steps in the process. Become a doer and get in the habit of taking more action. Even if you fear taking action, the process of doing is itself the best cure for fear. The most difficult time to take action is when doing something for the first time. Force yourself if you have to. Even if you don't know how to do something, once you start moving you'll begin to stimulate the flow of ideas and inspire yourself to continued action. After you put yourself into motion, you'll begin to build up your confidence and the fear will go away.

Six Qualities Required to Turn Words into ACTION

A—AFFIRMATION: Establish, verify, and announce your goals.
C—COMMIT: Commit to taking action on your goals.
T—TENACITY: Persist, create drive, and have determination.
I—INTUITION: Trust your inner feelings, insight, and sense of direction.
O—OPPORTUNITY: Open yourself up to chance, recognize your advantage, so you can grab on when your big break comes.
N—NEVER GIVE UP: Keep going until you reach your goals.

There is no point in beating yourself up over what you didn't do. Yet it is a good idea to take a look at the reasons why you didn't take action. See if you can figure out:

What gets in your way?
What stops you from doing what you say you want to do?

Maybe you don't want whatever it is badly enough, or maybe fear—of failure, of success, of the unknown—gets in the way. Yet whatever stops you from taking action also stops you from having the life that you truly deserve.

Here's a radical thought: Perhaps the reason you are *not* taking action is that this isn't the right time for you to do it. Maybe all you want or need to do right now is talk about it. Maybe right now it is more fun talking about taking action than actually taking it. Often the things we talk about are not actually the things we want to do anything about. If you truly wanted to take action, you wouldn't be sitting around talking about it; you would be doing something about it!

Action is the only way to make things happen. If there is something that you should do, but don't want to, stop talking about it and drop it. Be honest with yourself that this isn't the time or place and focus your energy on what you will and can do to move forward. As long as you are giving energy to something that you are never going to do, you won't have the energy to do what you want and will do. Your actions speak louder than words!

Having goals and affirming them to yourself and others who support your goals and dreams is important. Yet action is the principle missing in the process of achieving your goals and dreams.

Taking action turns dreamers into doers.

Today is the day you can get out of your head and onto your feet. Sitting on the couch and dreaming about what you want will not make it happen. Yet, converting your ideas into an experience will.

~ DEBBIE ALLEN
International Business Speaker, Author, www.DebbieAllen.com

I had to make my own living and my own opportunity!
But I made it! Don't sit down and wait for the opportunities to come.
Get up and make them!

~ MADAM C. J. WALKER
Creator of African-American hair care products and America's first black female millionaire

WHAT SPARKLES
YOUR INSPIRATION?

*W*hen you get sparkles of inspiration—where everything simply gels together for you—a moment where you have been able to get in touch with your intuition, have been given that wonderful piece of wisdom that you have been waiting for. This could be a simple realization about something significant to you in your life, or it could be a new idea you are open to pursuing. When you get this spark, it's important to recognize what was going on when it arose so you will be able to reach your intuitive wisdom again. When did you get that spark? Take a moment to look at the who, what, when, where, how.

Ask yourself:
How did that spark arise?
What was the environment like?
What activity was I doing?
Was there a specific person or support present?

That spark you've found represents a new seed inside you that you want to foster, nurture, and grow, so try this exercise on for size!

~ LIZ MYERS, M.A.
Rooted Living Coaching, www.RootedLiving.com

A candle loses none of its light by lighting another candle.
~ CHINESE PROVERB

Thirty Rules for
Women in Business

*M*y nieces, Marlo and Jada, were born September 9, 2004. Presuming they go to college, they will be in the work world in the year 2026, which seems an impossibly long time away. However, *tempus fugit* ("time flies" in Latin), and that time will come. Here's my advice for them, from what I've learned in more than twenty-five years in business as a fundraising professional and consultant.

1. Rejection isn't fatal. What are you going to do, curl up in a ball under your covers and never come out? Yes, it hurts, but it won't kill you. Never let the fear of rejection stop you from asking.

2. Set a monthly goal. You can pick any habit you want to break, or a habit you want to pick up, and set a goal around that habit. Since it takes about twenty-one days to make or break a habit, this will give you plenty of time. I start on the first of the month and write down my goal every day in my schedule book. I've used this to stop drinking coffee and to start exercising, to track my billable hours and to stop taking afternoon naps. It's very effective, and much better than making New Year's resolutions.

3. Know what you want to do with your time on earth and write it down. It's easier to say no to things that don't fit your goals if you know what those goals are.

4. Get a whiteboard for your office or anywhere you spend time. Write your goals on it, and update it frequently. Out of sight is out of mind, but if you look at it all the time, the things you write are at the foremost of your mind.

5. Learn technology. Don't be a dinosaur. Yes, it's changing fast, but change with it. If you don't know anything, go to a big-box technology store and start looking at products. If you don't understand something, ask someone around you.

6. The corollary to rule five is to set a budget for your technology. Figure you'll need a new computer or major computer upgrade every three years. You'll probably want a new cell phone every two years. There are things in your future that are unimaginable to you now, but I can assure you they'll cost money. Put it in your budget, and keep up with what's new so you know what to get.

7. Set an education budget as well. Go to conferences to stay updated in your field. Take new classes so you're learning something new every year. Certification in my profession requires this, and the world is moving fast enough that it's a necessity.

8. Dress a little better than necessary. You look like you're going up, and that's attractive to others.

9. Look for the chance to be someone's angel. Give blood, forward a job posting, pick up garbage at the beach, or visit a senior in a nursing home. Don't wait for the holidays to do something nice, look for opportunities to do it.

10. Pretend you're a philanthropist and think about what donations you would make if you inherited a billion dollars. Then, look for groups working in those areas, and give an amount within your budget. If you hold tightly to your money, you won't get more, but if you give it away, more will come to you.

11. When you're negotiating for a salary, say the amount you want and shut up. First to speak loses. If the other person says, "That's not in our budget," then you might not get that amount, but you'll probably end up getting something more. If you keep speaking

and say, "Unless of course that's too much," you won't get it. You can't get if you don't ask.

12. Don't assume a potential employer is telling the truth when he or she says, "We'll give you a raise in six months" or "You'll get an assistant." Ask them to put it in writing. If they say no, you'll know it was never true to begin with. Ask yourself if you're willing to work with someone who starts out by lying to you.

13. When interviewing for a job, ask how long the employees have been there, especially people in your position. If the last three people in your position were promoted, that's a good sign. If the last three lasted two years or less, no matter what the excuse, you know it's not a good place to work.

14. Don't badmouth previous bosses. The employer imagines what you'll say about them next.

15. It's better not to have romances at the office, but if you must, you get just one. After that, a second romance gives you a reputation. You need to look for another job if you want to have a second romance at work. Also, when it comes to romance, no one ever regretted waiting, but plenty of people regret going too quickly.

16. Keep your personal life at home. Be mysterious. Let them guess. No one really wants to know whom you're dating or what you do in your free time.

17. Don't come in late. The person who comes in to work late, rushed, and disheveled doesn't get any respect. It's easier to come in ten minutes early. You feel good; you're relaxed and ready to go.

18. Straighten up before you leave each day, and make a list of what needs to get done the next day. This lets you start the job quickly, without having to remember where you left off, and a tidy workspace leaves you relaxed while impressing others.

19. The person who is there early gets more respect than the person who stays late. Coming in early means you're eager to work, staying late means you need extra time to get things done and therefore might not be competent. That's only an opinion, and I was always the type to stay late.

20. Say "please" and "thank you," even to an assistant. Pay well and tip well. The people around you are responsible for your well-being and your reputation in the world. You'll never regret treating them well, even when no one is looking

21. Network, even when you're not looking for a job. If you forward potential jobs to others, they'll remember you. If you know what others are doing in your field, it benefits you.

22. Take vacations. Life is too short to work all the time.

23. Take care of your body. People who are fit, and those who eat well and exercise, work better and more productively.

24. Put yourself in the other person's shoes. Be quick to praise and slow to anger. Put praise in writing and criticize verbally in private. However, if you suspect you'll need to fire someone, be sure to document everything.

25. Set aside "Forget you!" money. If you have to, you can say to the boss, "Forget you! I don't need to work here" and be able to quit. Three months of savings in the bank, easily accessible, will let you stand up for yourself when you really must. (The phrase isn't quite "Forget you!" but that will have to do.)

26. Other people are more concerned with their lives than with yours: look for ways to make your boss's life easier and to be a good listener, and you'll always have work and friends.

27. Everyone gets fired; it's a fact of life. Learn what you can from it and then let it go.

28. Get a will! Having a will doesn't mean you'll die, and not having one won't keep you alive. In fact, people who have a will are shown to live longer. 70 percent of the population dies without a will, yet 70 percent of the people who die know a year in advance that it's the last year of their life. Don't let your fears or concerns hamper you, and don't leave it to others to figure out. Take responsibility for the closing of your time on earth.

29. There is abundance in the world. If you negotiate from a position of abundance, not scarcity, and deliver more than you are asked, then you will have more than enough in work, romance, and life.

30. Pay it forward. You have the responsibility to take the gifts you've been given to benefit others.

~ KATHERINE WERTHEIM, CFRE
Werth-It, www.werth-it.com

✦ ✦ ✦

When you reach an obstacle, turn it into an opportunity. You have the choice. You can overcome and be a winner, or you can allow it to overcome you and be a loser. The choice is yours and yours alone. Refuse to throw in the towel. Go that extra mile that failures refuse to travel. It is far better to be exhausted from success than to be rested from failure.

~ MARY KAY ASH
Founder of Mary Kay Cosmetics

The important thing is not being afraid to take a chance. Remember, the greatest failure is to not try. Once you find something you love to do, be the best at doing it.

~ DEBBI FIELDS
Founder of Mrs. Fields Cookies

AFFIRMATIONS FOR WOMEN IN BUSINESS

My career is my choice of service,
and my service is an extension of my love.
My career celebrates who I really am.
I am living my most pure essence, with ease and grace,
living creatively every project, task, and day.
I know in my heart "the right thing to do,"
and with integrity and respect, I do it.
I honor myself for my choices.
By aligning with my calling, I am living my
heart's desire and my higher purpose.
With ease and grace, I make decisions.
Business and opportunities flow abundantly to me, because I am
living my truth, living my passion, and living my calling.
I honor my body, listen to it, and nurture it.
Today and every day, I expect great things.
I open my heart, my mind, and my spirit to the guidance of God.
I am willing to see my magnificence.
I am willing to receive all abundant gifts from the Universe.
I graciously receive praise and prosperity.
I honor my path as well as the path of others.

~ SHERYL ROUSH
Inspirational Speaker, Entrepreneur, www.SparklePresentations.com
© 2008 Sheryl L. Roush

Every obstacle we encounter is a natural and necessary step on the road to achieving our dreams.
~ CYNTHIA KERSEY
Speaker, Author of Unstoppable, *www.unstoppable.net*

This is the day which the Lord has made; let us rejoice and be glad in it.
~ PSALM 118:24

Dreams build bridges between where we are now and where we can be in the future whether that means tomorrow, six months from now or ten years from now. Fueling our inner drive, they make our feet light, our tasks exciting instead of burdensome and our hopes infinitely possible.
~ JULIE JORDAN SCOTT

Always continue the climb. It is possible for you to do whatever you choose, if you first get to know who you are and are willing to work with a power that is greater than ourselves to do it.
~ OPRAH WINFREY

Whatever women do they must do twice as well as men to be thought half as good. Luckily, this is not difficult.
~ CHARLOTTE WHITTEN
Former Mayor of Ottawa

FERTILE SOIL FOR DREAMS

*F*rom my perspective, the field of "business" offers a woman fertile soil from which to create the future of her dreams. Being the owner of a business gives a woman the opportunity to draw on all of her natural intuitive, creative skills, while forcing her to develop the logical, left side of the brain as well. This definition of business goes directly against my youthful perception that business is a soulless, cut and dried, male-oriented field in which the bottom-line is the only "raison d'etre."

I slowly came to this realization after I became part owner of a small architectural/engineering company started by my husband in the mid-1980s. The company opened its doors about the same time we started our family. At first, my only goal as a business owner was to justify quitting my full-time job in the city. My real objective was to spend more time at home with my new baby. Nonetheless, I wanted to make myself useful at the company because that was what was economically supporting our entire family.

With an educational background in journalism and a professional background in public relations, I started my new career by writing marketing proposals and putting together written material about the company. I quickly learned what was effective and what was not and made adjustments accordingly. What a thrill it was to see new projects for the company that were the direct result of my planning, preparation and presentation! As more and more projects came in, we had to hire new staff, which meant we needed new equipment and then a larger office space. Once that was done, we needed to bring in more projects and so on.

What I had originally thought would be a boring occupation quickly became fascinating. I was a writer, a business strategist, a human resources specialist, a bookkeeper, a purchaser, and a public relations specialist. In essence, I became the heart and soul of this company, doing everything I could to keep it thriving. What had started out as a three-person company barely making enough money to pay the monthly bills turned into a thriving sixty-five person company with a portfolio of prestigious projects in the U.S. and abroad. No longer was I a one-person band doing all the non-technical tasks in order to keep the company viable. I became an executive who managed the work of others who were specialists in their fields. This experience challenged me beyond my wildest dreams and helped me grow both personally and professionally in ways I did not know were possible.

Being a business owner, particularly a business owner who has a spouse, poses its own set of challenges that are not always negotiated successfully. Such was my experience. After seventeen years, both the marriage and the business were dissolved. There are no regrets, however. The experience gained as a business owner is priceless. This is the legacy that I am giving to my three daughters who may or may not choose to pursue a career in business. But if they do, they will start off with the knowledge that being a businesswoman is one of the most challenging and rewarding careers they can pursue!

~ ELIZABETH BATEMAN
Director of Marketing, Cass, Sowatsky & Chapman Associates, www.csc-a.com

BE A DREAMER

*I*f you want something good to happen in your life, you must first start with a dream. Dream about what you want to achieve financially or the kind of marriage you want. Dream about that new car or that new addition to your home. Dream about that education for your children or that promotion you want to get.

Be a dreamer—is the first step toward making something happen. Back in the 1960s we came to know a man who was a dreamer. Many people disliked this man—many people disagreed with this man's dream. But nothing killed the dream.

Dr. Martin Luther King, Jr. stood firm. His voice rang out as he said: "I have a dream." Even though many disagreed with Martin Luther King, people of all races, of all countries have benefited because a man dared to dream.

What are your dreams? Do you allow yourself the opportunity to dream about the things you want in life? Everyday, give yourself the pleasure of dreaming. It is from your dreams that your realities begin. Today is your day for dreaming.

~ DR. ZONNYA
The First Lady of Motivation, Speaker, Author, www.drzonnya.org

❖ ❖ ❖

What if we're all meant to be what we secretly dream?
What would you ask if you knew you could have anything?
Like the mighty oak sleeps in the heart of a seed . . .
Are there miracles in you and me?
What would I do today . . . *If I Were Brave?*

~ JANA STANFIELD
Singer, songwriter, from the song "If I Were Brave," www.JanaStanfield.com

HERE'S YOUR KICK IN THE PANTS!

*E*verything starts with an idea. I hear so many people talk about how they want to start their own business, or do this or that. And it remains just that—talk. If you have an idea and you want to pursue it, then *do it*! What is holding you back? I bet most are just excuses—or a deep-seated fear of failure. If you *really* want to do it, there are few real obstacles. And you can start small . . . .

Everyone thinks they have to be an instant success. You can start something small, on the side. The necessary recipe for success includes the idea to do it and the energy and willingness to follow through and to do what it takes. The big question to ask yourself is this: Will I have regrets if I don't do this before I am too old to act upon my dreams? If the answer is yes, you better get out of your couch potato mode and start moving! If the answer is no, well, you are not yet motivated enough to translate your dreams into actions.

Take baby steps. Break your dream down into what is needed to make your dream real. Hang around others who are what I call "do-ers." They will energize you and give you the emotional support you need to move forward. Seek out help from your community. Read books and check the Internet for practical advice to create and grow a business. The information is out there on the how-tos.

The main thing is making a true decision to finally say *enough is enough*! *I am going to really do this thing*! Do your homework, do your research and do your best. Failure is a possibility in any new venture, but if you do your research well, you will set yourself up for a likely success. And how will you know the outcome unless you take the risk and go for it? So here's your kick in the pants, girl! *Dream It—Go For It—Do It!* Here's wishing you terrific success in acting on your dreams!

~ ANDREA GOLD
© 2008 Andrea H. Gold, www.GoldStars.com

I'M NOT FINISHED WITH ME YET

When you take a look at me
If you don't like what you see
Just remember in my
ways I am not set.
And if you don't think that I'm
Always perfect all the time
There's no need for you
to really get upset.
For I'm changing every day
In the things I do and say
And my attitude and
thinking better get.
So please be merciful and kind
And keep just one thing
in mind.
Just one truth:
I'm not finished with me yet.

When I take a look at you
And I don't like what you do
I'll remember in your
ways you're not set.
And if I don't understand
Every little thing you've planned
It may not be my business
So why should I get upset?
For you're changing every day
In the things you do and say
And your attitude, like mine,
I hope will better get.
So I'll be merciful and kind
And I'll keep just one thing
in mind.
Just one truth:
You're not finished with you yet.

Why settle for less,
When you can choose
To experience so much
More—Better—Greater?

~ DR. ZONNYA
The First Lady of Motivation, Speaker, Author
www.drzonnya.org

The Driving Force

GAMES MOTHER
NEVER TAUGHT ME!

*W*omen entering the workforce in the 1970s, especially those going into non-traditional jobs, were encouraged to read books like *Games Mother Never Taught Me*. The underlying message of most business books at the time told women that they must become more like their male counterparts in order to be more effective in their career. Women seemed to accept the fact that to get ahead, one must learn certain corporate "games."

The underlying assumptions were:

1. There were certain games played in all corporate settings.
2. Men knew about these games.
3. Women must learn these games in order to advance their career.

Women soon realized that they must work together to help each other learn basic survival skills. As a result, many companies sprouted women's committees in the 1980s. The goal of these committees was twofold:

1. To provide a mechanism for women to help each other with the challenges of living in a man's world.
2. To provide an avenue for women to be able to make recommendations to management on more effective utilization of women in the workforce.

The support groups were very effective in teaching women, both in traditional and non-traditional jobs, how to communicate more effectively within the context of corporate settings. Many resources, i.e., books, seminars, and workshops were created to achieve these goals. As a participant in many of these seminars and workshops, it still seems strange to me that general gamesmanship was accepted and discussed yet some very basic questions were never explored. In hindsight I wonder why the following questions did not come up for discussion:

1. *What is the name of the game we are playing?*
2. *What are the ground rules of the game?*
3. *How is success (winning) measured?*
4 *Who gets rewarded—individual achievers or teams?*

During the 1980s I was very much involved with setting up a career development center and administering corporate management training efforts in a large aerospace firm. From my observations, I don't think things really worked for women when they attempted to emulate their male counterparts. It felt like coming to work in a pair of shoes that were a size too small. You could function, but it never felt quite right. What was unfortunate was the fact that many women considered themselves less successful or failures because they could not (or would not) approach work exactly like their male peers. It took another decade before women and some enlightened men began to realize and appreciate the skills that women brought to the working environment.

However, it was not until the 1990s, when many organizations were suddenly thrust into "total quality" efforts, that challenges to the established way of doing business were presented. The problems encountered by the initial attempts at creating a "total quality" team environment came as no surprise. This was because the reward systems in most organizations did not change to accommodate new management practices. If management effectiveness continued to be measured by individual achievement, there was no incentive to change. However, it was during this time that women came to realize that they could function quite effectively in team settings.

In the early 1990s a major shift occurred in the way women approached the job. Rather than expend a lot of energy trying to be like men, women came to realize that they brought unique skills to the marketplace that fit very well into the new team-focused environment. Many successful women I had the privilege to work with during this time shifted their focus to restructuring the reward systems in organizations. Once the message was clear that managers and/or project leaders were accountable for the performance of their group, behavior changes from task orientation to process orientation occurred. It is my bias that affirmative action programs and the women's movement may have set the stage for working women; however it was the "total quality" movement, coupled with technological advances, that did more to effectively integrate women into the management ranks.

I remember working with a nationally recognized management consulting firm in the late 1990s on our corporate executive development and leadership programs and saying to myself, "It's about time." The content of the new leadership programs focused almost entirely on those skills that seemed to come more naturally to women. Whether social conditioning or genetics, women found it much easier to adapt their natural instincts to this new focus.

As the turn of the century rolled around and I was getting ready to leave the corporate world to venture out on my own, I felt a sense of peace and pride in the progress women had made during the last several decades. In the 70s women were primarily learners. In the 80s they became observers, and in the 90s they took on the role of challengers.

I believe I made some of the best hiring decisions during the last year with my organization. I remember interviewing two equally qualified candidates for a particular position, one male and one female. Both candidates did not have actual experience in one small aspect of the position. If this interview had been twenty years earlier, the female candidate would have offered to go to school to fulfill all the job requirements. However, today's female response was identical to her male counterpart. The young woman I interviewed responded as follows: "Even though I have not done this exact thing, I have performed similar tasks in the past and I am quick to learn new things on the job to keep pace with technology and other changes that might impact my effectiveness on the job." Hearing this young woman's response was music to my ears. She clearly understood the concept of "transferable skills." Rather than defining herself by previous jobs she had held, she was able to talk about the actual skills she utilized in her previous positions and how those same skills could be applied to the position she was seeking. She also convinced me that one of her hobbies required some of the same skills as the job she was applying for. I hired her and have tracked her career progression over the last few years. Not only was she very successful in the position, she also serves as an excellent role model for new employees.

In summary, not only have women made personal progress during the last few decades, they have also been a major driving force in helping organizations adopt a more "humanizing" approach to employee issues such as child care, eldercare, and sabbatical leaves. Today's business environment is such that "competent" people who are eager to learn will be in demand rather than worrying whether they are male or female. However, I cannot conclude my observations without smiling while I tell you that I don't think women will be reading *Games Mother Never Taught Me*. Instead women will be writing a book—perhaps titled *Games Mother Invented*. Yes, she will share the lessons in the book with her daughters and perhaps even her sons! All things are possible because my former organization, the male-dominated aerospace industry, just elected its new president, a woman!

~ MARIANNE MATHEIS, M.S.
President, Career Dimensions, www.changespeaker.com

❖ ❖ ❖

Women spend 80 cents of every dollar in the marketplace. We could be the most powerful force for economic and environmental change in the 21st century if we focused our money where it could make the biggest difference. If a million people did that, it would have a $1 billion impact.

~ DIANE MACEACHERN
Source: A greener planet begins under the kitchen sink

If you understand women's consumer DNA and implement strategies that ring with authenticity, you will improve all of your marketing efforts. If you make it women-friendly, you make it everybody-friendly.

~ JOANNE YACCATO
Source: The 80% Minority: Reaching the Real World of Women Consumers

THE NATURE OF LEADERSHIP AND PERSONAL AMBITION

Jane is the heroine of A Merger of Equals, *a smart, funny and inspiring novel about contemporary women and men trying to succeed in the business world. Jane is ambitious, brilliant, cynical, and determined not to let her gender stymie her in any way. Here's what she has to say midway through the story about her ambition to reach the top:*

I had wanted to be a huge success in the business world practically since I was a child. Now I asked myself why. What was the purpose behind what I was trying to accomplish?

I knew that part of what fueled my determination to succeed was my desire to prove I could to all the people who seemed to think otherwise or to want to stop me. Closed ranks drove me nuts. I hated being kept out or categorized or thwarted by expectations that had nothing to do with my personal competence or dedication. More than once, I had responded to "What motivates you?" by saying, "Because it's there and because I can."

Was I still trying to prove to my father that girls weren't second-class citizens? If so, who was that about? The world needs women among its leaders, and my successes would continue to have a positive impact on the availability of opportunities for other women, but wouldn't that be merely a side benefit of having proved that I, at least, didn't deserve to be overlooked?

I decided I had to recast my goal and my own sense of what motivated it. I had to sift out goals that were too personal, too exclusively about me. I wanted to become the kind of example that inspired other people and opened their eyes, not the kind they could effortlessly reject as self-serving or inimitable or out of the mainstream. It wouldn't be enough to carve out a foothold for myself or even to ascend to the top if the path I took erased itself behind me.

I wanted to throw my foothold and my path into high relief, to make them evident, difficult to reject and part of the regular fabric of business life. The changes I sought to bring about would become a reality only if and when people generally—other women to be sure, but, equally importantly, men—believed as a matter of course that a career like mine was just one more of many options routinely available to anyone with the talent and desire to pursue it—as opposed to something unusual for anyone other than a certain kind of man.

I wanted the women who came after me to have it easier, to feel a sense of comfort and welcome and belonging. I wanted them to have a better map and to experience less frustration along the way. I wanted them to feel less pressure to conform by renouncing part of the unique value they brought to the party—and, thus, denying the very differences that, used effectively, were their advantages.

The point I wanted to drive home was that you *could* be different and still succeed. Diversity—whether of gender, working style, personality, background or perspective—was the positive, the desirable business benefit, not something to be homogenized into invisibility.

I decided my real goal had to be to broaden the traditional profile, to make it more "normal" for someone other than the customary white male to roam the halls of corporate office buildings, be part of the official power structure and set the tone for business activity and cultural "truth." My vision was of a meritocracy where people could freely be who they were and succeed (or not) based on what they contributed. This, it seemed to me, was where the individual and organizational benefits of diversity intersected. And it was the altruistic crux of what was driving me.

I had also come to believe that it wouldn't do to give up anything important to achieve my success. Enormous personal sacrifice was neither necessary nor appropriate. Denying who I was or forgoing something I wanted or thought important so as to ease my climb to the top was a sucker bet.

What were the odds—really—that I would still be my whole self and capable of suddenly behaving as such if I'd spent decades pretending to be someone else? I was much more likely to become what I was pretending to be. And even if it were possible to remain whole while conforming to narrow-minded dictates, if I succeeded that way my message would effectively be "Pretend to be something you're not or you can't succeed." With that message, I wouldn't be much of an example—and I certainly wouldn't be a leader.

I wasn't looking to create yet another restrictive profile. I wanted to change the rules of the game by opening the doors. The only way to do that effectively was to succeed *by* being a whole person, my whole self—and, significantly, a woman.

Taking my gender off the table as an issue had served me well, but it was time to worry less that people *would* notice it and more that they would not.

~ DEBRA SNIDER
Speaker, Author
An excerpt from the novel A Merger of Equals, *www.DebraSnider.com*

THE NEW TRIPLE BOTTOM LINE AT WORK

"Care Counts" sounds like a trite phrase you would see on an elementary school fundraising bumper sticker— something next to the cupcakes at a bake sale. Perhaps that is why most people's eyes glaze over when they first hear me say it.

It could be a mother who, exhausted, counts the hours of lost sleep staying up caring for her baby last night. Or maybe it's a CEO who, upon hearing the word "count" thinks bottom line dollar value, and hearing the word "care" thinks "customer." It might also be an Olympian who is counting milliseconds shaved off their time, and cares about their Olympic gold. Whoever and wherever and whatever age or culture they come from, the people I work with from all walks of life don't really know what I mean when I say "Care Counts"—until they hear my story.

If I had known, when I was 19, what I mean now when I say, "Care Counts," I would have saved myself from hospitalizations, made my business and those of my clients profitable years sooner, averted thousands of dollars spent on therapy and graduate school and antidepressant drugs, would have reached hundreds if not thousands more people with the benefits of my work. Most of all I would have loved the moments of life lived and now passed that cannot be reclaimed in the stress and overcare that overcame me.

Are you no longer willing to settle for a schlock job that just pays your bills? Or are you not about to stand by in idle while watching a world collapse due to global warming? Yet, at the same time, are you unwilling to martyr yourself and your mouths to feed in endless volunteerism for some noble sake of the whole? On top of that, are you not willing to stress about the world, your bills, your health, and compromise your own life force in the process? If you answered yes to any of these questions, then congratulate yourself: you are part of a new economy, an economy with a triple bottom line.

The triple bottom line for doing business in a new era of globalization this:

1. *Is it fulfilling to me and good for my health and for my community?*
2. *Does it contribute to the planet and the environment?*
3. *Is it profitable and self sustaining?*

We are all part of one larger whole; there is no way that anything from a project, to a family, to a large scale business, can work well and last unless the answer is yes to all of these questions.

Worry, guilt, despair, overdrive, and other forms of care carried to an extreme hurt us, stress us out, and don't help others. Self-care is the absolute foundation to the new triple bottom line. But how do you care for yourself, and have a profitable business? For many, that seems like a contradiction! And then to add the environmental and global aspect of our triple bottom line? Sheesh! A tall order! If focusing on the whole world feels too big, it is enough to remember that your care for one person (even for yourself, if it is genuine!) extends beyond you in a ripple effect that can be measured, with impact potentially far greater than we know. Do you need special skills or tools or technology to do this? No!

One of my favorite examples of the new triple bottom line comes from a newspaper article called the "Rescuing Hug." A photo of premature newborn twins shows one twin with a yellow dot on her diaper, being hugged by her sister with a red dot on her diaper. Hospital policy had been for the twins to be in separate incubators.

Three months premature, the younger twin was dying. Her heart rate would not regulate, her temperature refused to rise to normal. On intuition, a nurse placed the older twin in her sister's incubator, and the older twin immediately, at three months premature, wrapped her arms around her sister in care. Within minutes, the younger twin's heart rate regulated, her temperature rose to normal, and both twins lived. Care counts.

If a premature infant can do it, anyone can. Care, true and genuine care, is our true nature, our birthright. It makes sense and it makes cents. Thanks to modern research, I can communicate to a harried mom that even if she does not do it perfectly, if her care is in it, it counts. I can prove to a CEO that if she creates a company where genuine care for her customers, her staff, and our environment is a top priority, it will show up in bottom line dollar benefit through increased sales, decreased turnover, and more efficient use of resources. I can help an Olympic athlete get that extra edge in her game by going for the gold not for her own self aggrandizement, but for the attention it will bring the causes that she cares so much about. Her care puts her in the zone of peak performance fast.

What is your triple bottom line? If you were the older twin, what would you wrap your arms around? I am on fire about your care, because your care counts. Your care can change the world in a heartbeat.

"It matters not what you do, only that you do whatever you do with love." -Mother Theresa

~ SHEVA CARR
Founding CEO, Fyera!, www.fyera.com

INVENTING WOMEN

*T*he history books are filled with hundreds of stories praising men of honor and valor who changed the course of his-story, and in comparison, there are just a handful of women mentioned who have made a difference. In searching the archives for women who have valiantly spoken up and changed the course of history equal to the likes of Abraham Lincoln, Thomas Edison, and Martin Luther King, I polled both men and women, "Name four men who radically changed history." Four names immediately came forth without hesitation. "That was too easy!" Then I asked, "Now, name four women who have equally changed history." "Wow, that's a hard one."

Everyone knows that Edison invented the electric light bulb; Alexander Graham Bell, the telephone; Henry Ford, the first automobile; and the Wright Brothers were the first to take to the friendly skies. Now, stop and take a moment to name three things invented by women. How did you do? When it comes to creating, women have come up with some amazing ideas that come from the heart such as:

The Paper Bag—Margaret Knight, 1861
Margaret received her first patent when she was thirty, for a machine that cut, pasted, and glued paper bags together. Even then she had to fight in court with a man who tried to steal her idea by stating that a mere woman didn't have the sense to invent such a machine. She won her case and went on to patent over twenty-two inventions.

Radium and Polonium Used in X-rays—Madam Marie Curie, 1887

Marie discovered the two radioactive elements, radium and polonium. She became the most famous woman in the world by the end of World War I, and in 1911, she won the first of two Nobel prizes.

The Dishwasher—Josephine Cochran, 1893
In 1886, Josephine proclaimed in disgust, "If nobody else is going to invent a dishwashing machine, I'll do it myself!" So she did, and founded a company that eventually became KitchenAid®. Unfortunately for her, the dishwasher did not catch on until the 1950s.

The Windshield Wiper—Mary Anderson, 1903
Mary received her first patent for a window cleaning device in 1903. By 1916, her invention was standard equipment on all American cars.

Satellite Communications—Hedy Lamar, 1941
For all of us over forty, the name Hedy Lamar may ring a bell. She was a movie star "pin-up girl" in the 1940s. She had both beauty and brains. The original purpose for her invention was to guide torpedoes by radio signal during World War II. She received a patent for her idea in 1941. When the patent expired, Sylvania modified it slightly and used her Secret Communications System for satellite technology.

Scotchguard®—Patsy Sherman, 1952
Patsy, a research chemist at 3M, discovered Scotchguard when a glass bottle containing a batch of latex mixture was accidentally dropped on an assistant's canvas shoe. She was inducted into the National Inventors Hall of Fame in 1983.

Liquid Paper®—Bette Nesmith Graham, 1956

Originally called "mistake out," this handy invention came out of the need to cover up the mistakes of a secretary. Using art materials in her kitchen, Bette created a product that every secretary in her building wanted to buy. With her nine-year-old son, Michael Nesmith, she bottled and filled orders. By 1967, these humble mother and son beginnings had grown into a million dollar business. In 1980, Bette sold the business for $47.5 million and died six months later. Oh, by the way, if the name Michael Nesmith sounds familiar, it's because he is one of the original members of The Monkees, a popular 70s singing group. "Here we come . . . ."

Before the 1840s, women were not even allowed to hold a patent in their own name, so all of the inventions created by women had to be filed with a man's name. He, of course, got the credit and his own chapter in his-story. I wonder how many of the inventions we use today were invented by women and hidden under the assumed name of a man in order to obtain a legal patent?

Could it be that Mrs. Graham Bell or Mrs. Thomas Edison had their feminine fingers somewhere in those two creations? We may never know, but it's kind of fun to think about it. At present, statistics show that 20 percent of all inventions are from the creative minds of women, and the number is projected to reach 50 percent over the next generation. "You go, girl!"

~ JONI WILSON
Speaker, Singer, Voice expert, Author, www.JoniWilsonVoice.com
© 2005 Joni Wilson. From A Woman's Guide to Finding Her Voice in a Malevolent World

BE THE ONE YOU ARE

*D*uring my last year at college I signed up for a summer job in sales. After a short training program with a dozen young men I proudly took off to meet with my prospective clients hoping for fabulous commissions. But, I seemed to have no success at all – I hardly made any sales and I couldn't understand why. I had followed the training so well and done everything right.

After a few days it suddenly it dawned upon me: But of course! I was different. The sales training was given by a macho man, for a group of macho men. I was a girl! No wonder the training didn't produce results for me. I was petite, feminine and soft spoken. Me, making a macho presentation? I wasn't even believable to myself!

From that moment on, I changed. I began to Be ME. A Woman With Feelings. Asking my prospects about their families, health and hobbies... things I was interested in anyway. And I noticed my prospects liked my interest in them more than hearing about the many benefits of the product. And it paid off.

As the summer was over and I was going back to college, I had made much more money than any one else in the group... I had also won the achievement prize of the highest sales returns: An exclusive shaving/razor set for men!

But my biggest reward was that I had learned a sales secret: My success had come only because I dared be the one I am - instead of a poor copy of someone or something else.

I have found that the biggest success comes to those who are true to themselves. If you are a man or a woman, Chinese, or American, doesn't matter. Just be the one you are Because- we are all incredible powerhouses. We all come in different forms and shapes And this is good. It's the way it was meant to be.

~HELENA STEINER-HORNSTEYN, DD
Speaker, Singer, Voice expert, Author of Constant Awakening
www.SpeakingToYourHeart.com

Fulfilling Your Soul

WOMEN SUPPORTING WOMEN

*A*s more women (and men) become aware of the ideals of the Feminine Consciousness, or Sacred Feminine, one revolution of thought that might change the face of our planet and society for the better, is that they realize that women are being called upon to be the visionaries, venturers, and vessels of change. Women can no longer be satisfied as the primary hands that rock the cradles. Women must begin to think in terms of positioning themselves to be the hands that broker the deals that change the direction of society and shifting cultural norms. And as women come into more positions of influence and power, that does not mean simply a shift to women in charge who adopt the dominator, survival of the fittest business methods of our male counterparts, sometimes called "patriarchy in a skirt." Instead women must bring their inherent way of being in the world. They must bring ideals of partnership, compromise, negotiation, and the needs of the many rather than the few. It also means looking at the destructive and negative behaviors of women toward other women learned in our patriarchal society and making a conscious effort to have women support each other.

Women Are Wired Differently

Professor, writer, researcher, and psychologist, Carol Gilligan, the founder of "difference feminism," whose theories on women's moral development are a combination of a Freudian theme mixed with the theories of noted psychologists, Lawrence Kohlberg and Jean Piaget, inspired pop culture books on the difference of gender communication such as John Gray's *Men Are From Mars and Women Are From Venus*. Gilligan determined that women and men have different approaches when making decisions about morality. The basis for her research is women generally make decisions based on ethics of responsibility and care of self and the social environment rather than the male point of view reflecting what the rules are, ethics of justice, self-fulfillment, and personal rights. Before this influential feminist revelation changed thinking and caused a tidal wave of research and scholarship, (including new ways of encouraging girls' voices in art, education, and cultural projects) psychologists researching moral theory were usually men. Men seldom took women's perspective seriously because they were considered less developed or sophisticated as a result of not conforming to the standards of psychological expectation. Consequently, Gilligan believes the conclusions of the theorists were not accurate without women's voices considered in these evaluations.

But Women Thwart Each Other
Rather than Support Each Other

While women are wired to care more about the needs of the many than men are, women have still gone off track as Phyllis Chesler discusses with brilliance and stunning honesty in her book, *Women's Inhumanity to Women*. Chesler discusses the dynamics women employ to hurt and thwart each other. She brings attention to the elephant sitting in the living room so that the female gender might see what is being practiced in hopes they might become more reflective of their actions and begin down the road toward healing themselves and supporting their sisters. While many women only openly admit oppression of women by men, Chesler states, "To the extent that women are oppressed, we have also internalized the prevailing misogynist ideology which we uphold both in order to survive and in order to improve our own individual positions vis-à-vis all other women."

Women employ insidious and indirect methods of aggression toward one another and children. She cites cliques as being the female equivalent of bullies and lists the mean spirited maneuvers of name-calling, insulting, teasing, threatening, criticizing, and starting rumors as ways adult women and young girls are inhuman to one another. They shut each other out, gossip, break confidences, and become friends with another to get revenge on a former friend, or encourage others to dislike the person whom they are at odds with at the moment. Of course this is not the blueprint or sole mold for the make-up of the female gender, but Chesler's data showed women who performed in these ways were usually suffering from low self-esteem, lacked optimism, were dissatisfied with their lot in life and had a higher objectified body consciousness compared to women who were not hostile to one another. In other words, these women did not like themselves very much and projected that disappointment and anger toward others around them. It would be too easy to blame this negative attitude on women's systematic oppression over the years, but it certainly must be a causative link.

What might come as a surprise—especially in light of the strides made in women's rights and their advancements in society—is that it seemed women did not trust each other easily, preferring a woman homemaker to a career-oriented woman and when in the workplace, women who practiced male leadership styles. That might say a lot about the probability for the election of a woman president anytime soon. Women who were interviewed discussed the lack of trust among women with some saying their mothers instilled this mistrust within them. Another woman cited this as being a method perpetuated by men, of alienating women from one another. The intention being that women of the community would be less likely to compare notes and know what was really going on around them. So it seems neither gender can be assigned absolute responsibility for women's failure to trust each other.

Readers should not draw the conclusion that women hate each other; more accurately they idealize or demonize each other, much the same as the ways attributed to men. But this hostile behavior should be looked at because in some circumstances women say they do not *believe in* aggression but they *act* aggressively. Chesler believes "this disassociative capacity might prove quite resistant to the acknowledgment that aggression is wrong, even while continuing to act in aggressive ways, when girls, even more than boys, may be learning to disassociate themselves from any negative thing they do and deny that they have done it, even to themselves." And without the ability to admit wrong-doing, it could prove difficult to change the behavior.

Dominator Culture of Patriarchy Affects All Our Lives

We have been living in a "dominator culture" for thousands of years where the few at the top benefit from the toil and subjugation of the masses at the bottom of the heap. Those at the top of the hierarchical ladder of a dominator culture exercise fear, divisive and power tactics over those on the lower rungs of the ladder. Riane Eisler (*Chalice and the Blade*) cites Jean Baker Miller who notes "how the so-called need to control and dominate others is psychologically a function, *not* of a feeling of power but rather of a feeling of powerlessness." Distinguishing between "power *for* oneself and power *over* others," she writes: "The power of another person, or group of people was generally seen as dangerous. You had to control them or they would control you. But in the realm of human development, this is not a valid formulation." Miller explains the opposite is actually true. "In a basic sense, the greater the development of each individual the more able, more effective, and less needy of limiting or restricting others she or he will be."

Just a few of the undesirable characteristics of a dominator paradigm are: male dominance, ranking, manipulation, hoarding, co-dependency, left-brain thinking, fear tactics, violence against others, war, negative conditioning, alienation, exploitation, secrecy, coercion, scarcity, short term thinking, conquest of nature, and conformity. Addictions to abusive relationships are another telltale characteristic.

Femininity is viewed as indirect and manipulative and devalued. "Wedge issues" are developed to divide people and create an atmosphere where those who are unlike you become "alien or other" and as a result, can be deemed less-than or without value. When the Church of Spain sent missionaries into Peru to convert "the natives" after their conquest, the indigenous people were not even considered human by many of the people making the decisions about the fate of this once advanced and flourishing culture. They had a different god, looked different, spoke another language, therefore it was easy to dismiss them and render them of little value. Dominator cultures do not really embrace the richness of diversity or the wisdom of tolerance. People are expendable cogs in a wheel.

But There Is Hope for Change

According to Malcolm Gladwell in his book, *The Tipping Point*, "What must underlie successful (social) epidemics, in the end, is a bedrock belief that change is possible, that people can radically transform their behavior or beliefs in the face of the right kind of impetus. In the end, Tipping Points are a reaffirmation of the potential for change and the power of intelligent action. Look at the world around. It may seem like an immovable, implacable place. It is not. With the slightest push—in the right place—it can be tipped."

And more and more people are beginning to realize that the ideals of the Sacred Feminine are the direction they are aiming for in this urgently needed and sought-after shift.

Science is beginning to explain how we can co-create our futures by our own thoughts. While we might currently remain cogs in the wheel, we must also exercise foresight and make more correct and conscious choices in our everyday, social, and political lives. We must take responsibility for our own education. We must vote. We must volunteer. We must put the right energy out there in the world.

Considering the thousands of years of patriarchy, we have made outstanding progress over the last decades. We have more people than ever before in public speaking about partnership. We are moving toward less rigid hierarchical organizations. As women have entered the work force, management consultants are citing the roles of managers as shifting to more of a facilitator or supportive role. Individuals on teams are allowed to "run with the ball" using their creativity, experience, and talents—with micro-managing becoming less the norm—resulting in goals being achieved in a co-created atmosphere rather than a power-over atmosphere. Carol Gilligan is quoted as saying, "The women's movement is taking a different form right now, and it is because it has been so effective and so successful that there's a huge counter-movement to try to stop it, to try to divide women from one another, to try to almost foment divisiveness."

continued on next page

Women Are Catalysts to Change the World

Women must heal themselves before they can change the world. We have probably all heard this before, but it bears repeating until every woman hears it, understands it, and walks that talk. Many believe women will be the major catalysts encouraging change toward a more balanced society. That being said, we have much work to do with our sisters and daughters, families, friends, lovers, fathers and brothers towards more partnership-oriented relationships at home, at work, and in our government. It is not enough that we just seek gender equality and true partnership with men. Women just learn to actively and consciously support other women. And both genders must strive to be in service rather than being in power because with service comes care and humility and too often with power comes corruption.

All of the aforementioned scholarly works describing these behaviors or paradigms deserve a more in-depth look; however, these concepts, alone or in tandem, might offer insight into the inherent difficulties in partnerships of all kinds, not just between women. These authors and scholars are certainly giving us a mirror for self-reflecting if we will only look with objective eyes. They have courageously placed detour signs along the avenues we have been traveling. It is up to us if we are going to continue along familiar paths or are we willing to risk taking another road toward a different destination called partnership!

~ KAREN TATE
Speaker, Author, Radio Show Host, www.KarenTate.com
Excerpt from Walking An Ancient Path: Rebirthing Goddess on Planet Earth

HEALING THE SEPARATION BETWEEN PHYSICAL ABUNDANCE AND FULFILLING YOUR SOUL

*M*any of us tend to make basic assumptions when we think about business, which are not necessarily true, and represent an old paradigm view of how survival and abundance are obtained. Generally we define business as how we earn our living. Most people spend the majority of their day doing unfulfilling things in order to earn it. This is because in the old framework there is a separation between what's necessary to do to survive on the physical level, and what matters to us on a soul level.

What causes this separation between the physical and the soul level has to do with a division or splitting off within the self, resulting in the creation of a substitute self. The substitute self is formed, on an unconscious level in early life, in the areas in which we made limiting decisions such as: "Who I am is not valuable," "I am bad," "I can't have what I really want," etc. These decisions are always some form of deciding there is some fundamental defect or fault in our self and in the way life works. We then separate our awareness from the part of our self we judged against and which we decided can't be fulfilled in life, and we bury that part deep in our unconscious, in an effort to get rid of it. And then we begin building a substitute, "more acceptable" and less vulnerable self (the ego self) with which to get by out in the world. This substitute self is focused on goals that symbolize, but are only substitutes for, what we really desire. The substitute self lives in an alternate world, which is generally defined by and limited to what it thinks it can control. That self is disconnected from present-moment experience, which is where real nourishment or fulfillment can be accessed. And it separates us from our God-self—our higher self, our soul.

The limiting decisions, which cause the division within the self, are what cause us to believe there has to be a separation between what really matters to us on a soul level, and what is necessary in order to physically survive. Many of these limiting decisions are shared by humanity in general. The result of this frequently shows up for people in middle-age, known as "mid-life crisis." It occurs when the person becomes aware that the life they have spent so much time, energy, and resources in building up (particularly in their career) has nothing, or very little, to do with what really matters to them.

But there is no inherent conflict between fulfilling ourselves on a soul level and living a life filled with physical abundance. However in the new paradigm, there are entirely different principles, than in the old one, for how one succeeds in whatever one does or in whatever one desires, including physical abundance. In the new paradigm, the world of spirit leads and the world of the physical follows that spiritual lead. Because the physical world is finite and the world of spirit is infinite, this shifts us from a limited world, with limited possibilities, to a world of infinite possibilities and infinite resources. In the unlimited world of spirit, the foundation is love, and exists outside of the framework of controlling, or winning, or any form of competition.

This type of success is dependent upon the support of the universe (or, depending upon your belief systems; Life, God, Spirit, the Divine . . .). The Divine is where the source of our survival and well-being actually lies, and is a larger framework than any immediate, conceived of goal. What is required for abundance in the new paradigm is to be in alignment with the Divine flow. Our immediate goals cannot be reached when their focus is not in alignment with the Divine flow.

The rule of thumb is that the universe is filled with resources, and what keeps us from connecting to these resources is when we have our channels for receiving them closed because of limiting decisions. In the closed state we can't see the resources right in front of us, and we limit ourselves to a very small frame of reference, therefore separating us from the Divine source and flow. The more we work through our unhealed issues, the more likely the channels will be open for our success and fulfillment in all areas of life.

Another important element in succeeding in the new paradigm is following our inner guidance. We each have inner guidance. It comes from a deeper source than our ego mind, and comes from a larger perspective than our immediate physical circumstances. It can align us with Divine wisdom, enabling us to play our part in a larger, evolutionary process. We may not start out with an awareness of our guidance, or recognize it when it communicates to us; but to participate in the new paradigm, it is crucially important to develop an awareness of it, as well as the faith and willingness to follow it. Making that leap of faith enables us to shift to a present in which there is no longer any conflict between our physical well-being and survival, and the fullest expression of who we are and what our soul is longing to express moment-to-moment in our lives.

~ JANE ILENE COHEN
Spiritually based Intuitive, Transformational Counselor, www.janecohen.net
© 2008 Jane Ilene Cohen

FINANCIAL ALCHEMY: CREATE A
NEW RELATIONSHIP WITH MONEY

*Y*our current financial situation is a direct reflection of your inner relationship with Money. If you don't like your finances, something needs to change in your relationship. This is where alchemy comes in.

Alchemy is the art of transformation. With roots in ancient Egypt and classical Greece, alchemy comes from a time when there was no distinction between science and magic. The mysteries of matter and consciousness were inextricably linked (as they are again, in today's quantum physics). These ancient studies gave birth to modern medicine, psychology, chemistry, and even Sir Isaac Newton's work on gravity.

The ultimate pursuit of alchemy was the "Philosophers' Stone," a substance believed to turn worthless metals into gold. While alchemists through the ages slaved in the laboratory, their metalwork concealed a spiritual process, a Philosophers' Stone that had to be kept hidden from the church: this was the process of *inner* transformation. Two principles are involved here: 1. turning lead into gold was an outer demonstration of inner transformation, and 2. the seed of the solution (the gold) was hidden in the problem (the lead). Use this article to discover your own Philosophers' Stone—your key to wealth and inner transformation—hidden in your relationship with Money.

Now, let's review guidelines I adapted from alchemist tradition.

Rule #1: As it is above, so it is below.

What shows up in your head is going to show up in your life. You will be using fundamental relationship coaching skills to help you transform your relationship with money from a dead seed into a flowering garden. A seed comes to life as a living, thriving, fruit-flowering plant . . . in the right environment. So, too, your own prosperity. Your potential for financial abundance is there, waiting for the necessary environment within you. Your relationship with money is like the soil that feeds or starves your economic growth. As long as you have hidden beliefs that cause you to unconsciously repel money, perhaps "protect" yourself from wealth, your garden will not grow.

Rule #2: There is no scarcity.

A wealthy client once explained to me how he had overcome poverty. "The amount of money out there in play every day is limitless, beyond our comprehension. Money is everywhere," he explained. And it's available in proportion to "how big your funnel is to take it in." He had learned to tap into the Source. This relationship supported him.

Rule #3: Consciousness gives you choice.

Even a small change in your relationship consciousness can have a huge impact on your material life. You get what you choose, but first you need to know what you're choosing. How do I know this? I experienced this transformation myself. For years I was struggling as a life coach. I had trouble attracting clients who would pay the fee I wanted. I found myself avoiding discussions of money as long as I could. The whole subject embarrassed me, and my discomfort translated into making clients uncomfortable too. I was "doing" all the right marketing things—networking, newsletters, sample sessions—and getting nowhere. I was not making a "grown-up" living. What was in my way, I wondered? My coach and I took a look at my relationship with Money. What were my stories about Money? What is this entity I'm in relationship with? What's going on with this relationship?

Two discoveries popped out: money didn't feel safe or reliable, and money caused separation. My family of origin would swing between being rich and poor over and over again, and money was a "reason" for family members not to talk to each other for decades. If my experience of money were given personhood, he'd look like an unkempt, unappealing, Hell's Angel biker type I didn't want to be around . . . someone untrustworthy who liked to cause fights. No wonder I wasn't bringing Money into my life!

This was not the relationship with Money I wanted to have (and it wasn't the relationship I wanted to model for my clients either). So I created a new paradigm. I fired the Biker persona and put a romantic, clean-cut, soft-spoken suitor in his place. I chose a new Money "person" to relate to. This Money was like a sweet boyfriend who wooed me with gifts. He even wore a tux! Whenever I received a check, signed a new client, came across some unexpected income, I would graciously thank Money for the lovely gift. And this version of Money was valued and invited into my life.

From then on my business and income kept growing. Within six months I had accrued such a waiting list of clients that I had to add group coaching to my services. I didn't have to look for my new clients; they were finding me, and all I had changed was my inner dialogue with money.

Now it's your turn: When you want to improve your financial situation, you must first uncover the beliefs that shaped your relationship with Money. Get out some paper and respond to these questions. (Writing creates clarity and speeds your change.)

What did you hear about money when you were growing up?
What beliefs get between you and prosperity?

Next, look at how Money has shown up in your life and in the lives of those around you. Give Money personhood in relationship to you. If Money were a person, what would your version of this Money "person" be like?

Who is Money?
How do you feel about Money?
Do you trust Money? Does Money trust you?
How does Money operate in your life?
How does Money feel about you?
Is Money someone you'd want to have a relationship with if you
*   didn't "have to?"*

Now, take a step back and imagine looking at this relationship between yourself and Money-as-a-person from the outside.

What shift needs to happen in this relationship?

Now, as yourself, negotiate with Money:

Does Money have a request for you?
Do you have a request for Money?
What's going to be different?
How do you want to be different in this relationship?
What is the next step to making this change real?

Money is like any other relationship; it comes where it's invited and appreciated. It rarely comes when it is chased. It can be your partner if you listen to it. The more you care for this relationship, the more money you will attract.

Three Final Tips

1. Appreciate money! When a penny shows up on the sidewalk, thank Money for the gift. Don't worry about denomination; appreciate everything. Think of how good *you* feel when you are valued for even a small gesture. It's the same for Money. Every time you practice receiving and appreciating, you train the universe to send you more. Show the universe what you value.

2. By now your capacity to receive is growing. You'll notice other stuff creeps in to limit the flow through your funnel to abundance. This stuff may look like clutter, broken appliances, old e-mails, toxic people, time wasters, or other energy drains. Clean house! Make space for what you want by having the courage to release what you don't want. You teach the universe how you want to be treated with every choice you make. And nothing gets the universe's attention like saying "No." It's your quickest ticket to miracles.

3. The most important place to make space for what you want is in your head. Clean out fear and pessimism. Plant love and trust instead. Your thoughts are your seeds, and you can grow flowers or weeds. What do you choose to grow?

~ MORGANA RAE
Master Results Coach, CPCC, MPNLP, Charmed Life Coaching,
www.CharmedLifeCoaching.com
© 2004-2008 Morgana Rae

A LEAP OF FAITH
Sometimes, simply by sitting, the soul collects wisdom.
~ ZEN PROVERB

A dozen years ago, I had a transformative encounter with what I call "divine energy" that changed me forever! Although others thought I was extremely fortunate and had a brilliant career, I felt nothing. That night as I sat and contemplated suicide once again, I suddenly realized that I wanted to make a difference in people's lives—to do something lasting and worthwhile.

In that one amazing moment, I knew my life purpose. I saw it outlined along with insights into my highest probable path. Immediately, my doubts tried to erase the vision by reminding me that I had no idea how to start over. That is when the most amazing awareness swept over me . . . Somehow, I had activated the ability to communicate directly with my Spiritual Source! Using this marvelous two-way communication, I started cleaning up the mess I had made of my life and set out to build a wonderful and more fulfilling life.

I began to pray and meditate—whenever and wherever—for any length of time. New-to-me methods and processes were downloaded to me empathically. I tested these thoughts rigorously, and they always produced tangible, practical results that ultimately created the framework of my present work as a spiritual coach. I was constantly provided with wisdom on how to live life to the fullest. No, I do not have special, arcane powers, but yes, we all have the ability to activate divine energy. I know because I have helped many others replicate my findings, too. Every day, I see its powerful ripple effect in all of our lives!

Peace on Earth will emerge from our deepest levels of sharing and caring about what we all choose to do and be, here and now, not from the superficial roles we assume in everyday life. Facades conceal our spiritual being. We need to recognize and honor the spiritual being that is the authentic you and me. That is why I am sharing my story with you.

I could say that after my initial mystical encounter, I ran out and immediately became a spiritual coach, but it did not happen that way. After my spiritual healing, I jumped headfirst into the study of spiritual, metaphysical, and healing philosophies, and became convinced that I was not the only one seeking a new life. This search made me even more determined to heal my life and create a better future that would produce everything I needed or even wanted. Healing and prosperity are the same to me—a progressive process. I discovered that *by chance* I could easily find books with the answers I sought or *by chance* meet people who would immediately help me. Using my own two-way communication with the divine more and more, I *received* immediate in-depth answers to my most pressing problems! Suggestions, affirmations, exercises, plus what I called "divine prescriptions," came easily to me whenever I prayed. Each time, I trusted and implemented these *prescriptions*, my life changed. I began sharing them with others until they, too, saw their lives improve!

My husband and I had been trying for several years to have a child, and at one point I remember praying about getting pregnant. The response was, "Let go of your need to have a baby." We then agreed that if we never had a child, we would still be happy. We acknowledged that our happiness did not hinge on having children, and that if we did not have any, we would find other outlets for our parental love with nieces and nephews. One month later, I was pregnant!

When I was eight months pregnant, I remember writing in my journal, "What am I going to do when the baby is born since I want to serve God always? How can I do that and still make a good living?" I had asked this before and not received any specific answer. The now-familiar sensation that I get when on the receiving end of this two-way spiritual communication process began, and a flood of words poured through my pen onto the paper. "This would be a good time to open a coaching practice. Call it *A Choice for Joy!* Name your baby Joy, dedicate your coaching work to the Holy Spirit . . . and trust!" I remember staring at the paper thinking that this had to be a fantasy.

The next day, my mentor and teacher, Ruth Lee, handed me a magazine to read. She gave no instructions other than that it contained what I needed to know, and to read it cover-to-cover if necessary. Upon opening the magazine, I felt goose bumps and shivers unrelated to my advanced pregnancy. Tears streamed down my face as I read a headline: "Create a Life of Your Dreams—Be a Coach!" *I just knew* this was how I would create a better life—one of prosperity and divine inspiration! The article explained in detail the profession of coaching, a new idea at the time.

Amazed to read about what I had previously *received* through journaling my Divine Guidance System, I nevertheless struggled to believe that coaching others could be my career, too. The author listed organizations that offered training and mentioned a virtual university where you could take classes via phone, which was perfect for a mother with a newborn.

With joyful expectation, I wrote in my journal: "Is this in my highest good to do this?" Struggling to write down the answer fast enough, I saw: "This is a good option. They will teach you the mechanics of creating a business, but *we* say you will go to this organization for reasons having nothing to do with the organization." I found that puzzling, but before fear could overcome me, I had a flashback to the night I had been healed. I remembered hearing, "One of your highest probable paths is to work with Workers of the Light . . . to help them release ego-concerns and connect with inner guidance, and *trust!*"

With a deep sense of *just knowing* that this would be my next step, I imagined how I would explain to my husband that I would not be going back to my executive position and would lose my high salary. When I told him *what I got* in my two-way communication, he smiled and said, "So you're finally ready to commit to doing what you love? It's about time!"

At that moment, I knew something significant had changed within me, but would I allow myself to totally trust my spiritual guidance? What lay in store for me if I did? All I can say now is that it made no rational or logical sense to do it then, but I *knew* it was right! Never before had I had such a powerful inner knowing. It was exhilarating and scary at the same time, but I felt total peace. That inner power catapulted me into an incredible life that has surpassed my previous dreams—a life of love, joy, and prosperity. It is a life dedicated to serving and helping others awaken that same power within themselves! You cannot discover this work in a linear way. It has to come to your mind from your Spiritual Source!

~ SHARON WILSON
Founder, Coaching from Spirit Institute, LLC
www.CoachingFromSpirit.com
Reprinted with permission from Chicken Soup for the Soul: Life Lessons for Mastering the Law of Attraction

FINDING YOUR NICHE

*F*inding your niche is fulfilling your life mission in your own unique way. It is a way that brings you greater appreciation and awareness of the present. It strengthens your sense of self-esteem. And it fulfills you.

Finding your niche is a matter of opening up to what you want in your heart. To know what you want in your heart, you must be able to feel what it's trying to tell you. To be able to feel it you must remove the judgments surrounding your experiences.

Many begin finding their niche at midlife. Some have known their niche all along but let their filtered perceptions of how one should live get in the way. This is the cause of the classic mid-life crisis. A person goes through life according to the perceived values that are assimilated throughout early life. When life no longer seems as if it will go on forever, or the person faces a traumatic change in lifestyle, a mid-life crisis is triggered, causing the person to re-evaluate priorities.

For example, let's say you are now working at a job that pays well enough to offer some financial stability. Let's say you are a department supervisor at a marketing firm. It's easy for you because you've been in the business a long time and you know your work backward and forward. Co-workers and the clients you work with acknowledge and accept your position within the work environment and business world. The work is familiar to you and you are comfortable with it.

Yet deep inside you really want to do something else. You know you would really rather be working on that idea for a video documentary you've had in mind for a number of years, but you can't seem to find the time. You fantasize about doing it but it never materializes. You haven't made it a priority.

You have judgments that prevent you from making the change:

"It would be irresponsible to just quit my job and do that."
*"I don't have time to work it in, and I can't quit what I'm doing
     now until there's enough money to do it."*
"It would be selfish."
"I'm not good enough at that."
"I don't have the connections."
"Life was never meant to be easy."

Your mind will continue to come up with reasons why you should never change what you are doing because what you are doing is familiar, even if it's not working for you financially or providing a sense of personal fulfillment. The subconscious aspect of mind loves what is familiar. It is the great storehouse of the familiar, a virtual library of information recording every memory, every learning experience, every emotion and every bit of data you have ever been exposed to that could be used as a benchmark against which to gauge the present or to fertilize your imagination at any time, now or in the future.

Years go by and suddenly you realize life is getting behind you. The years ahead don't seem to offer unlimited opportunities for procrastination anymore. Your energy level is not what it used to be and you notice the skin of your face and neck beginning to sag. Yet you continue to do the same thing, mindlessly hoping that something will come along to change your world for you.

The super-conscious mind, which inspires from a more trans-dimensional awareness, keeps pushing us to change in spite of ourselves. It plants the seeds of restlessness that desire to know more, to become more.

Then one day something happens. You get a phone call with some devastating news that shakes your world. Or maybe you find yourself in bed recovering from an accident or sudden health crisis. And then your world does begin to change. You begin to re-evaluate all your priorities. You realize the niche you've been filling feels more like a sinkhole than a position from which to explore your talents and interests. Spirit has stirred within you and awakened you to the messages of your heart. You realize it's time to get going. The value of being alive has taken on a new and greater importance. You begin to search for more meaning in the things you do every day. The seeds of restlessness have finally begun to sprout and grow back toward the light.

Suddenly the compost of life's past experience stored in the subconscious mind becomes the fertilizer for the newly sprouted seeds pushing to the surface of conscious awareness. By releasing judgments attached to past experiences, the experiences themselves become fertilizer for a richer life. By releasing judgments about what the self is feeling, compassion for all takes its place. Like a flower shooting up through compost, it is often through the rotting decay of an emotional wasteland that the blossom of Spirit asserts itself.

But why wait to be bombarded with change in such a cataclysmic way when you have the option to go for it right now with less stress? Your super-conscious has been nudging you all along the way.

~ MOONSTONE STAR WHITE
Speaker, Author, www.SpiritWindPublishing.com
Excerpt from *High Way From Hell, Using Emotion to Fan the Fire of Enlightenment*
© 2007 Moonstone Star White and Spirit Wind Publishing

Polishing Up on Business Skills

WHICH WORDS? BRING ELOQUENCE
TO YOUR PRESENTATION SKILLS

*E*loquence is lean. But, I didn't know that when I started speaking 7 years ago. I used weighty language, and for the wrong reasons. In retrospect I can see innocence in the mistake. I was a woman and often younger than my mostly male clients. My expertise had been acquired through an eclectic route and bore no degrees or designations to fortify surety in myself. So I used three-dollar words to sound credible, content-full, and smart. The more nervous I got, the more tiles disappeared from my scrabble bag.

A breakthrough came while a consultant was preparing me for a radio interview on parenting, the topic of which was to be a concept I call "The Trophy Child." In our practice session, I kept saying the problem of using our children to gain status was *systemic*, and she kept saying the word *systemic* was inaccessible and preventing me from connecting with the audience. She was right and this "a-ha" led to the development of a mental filter. A little bell began to go off when the wrong motive was behind a lavish word. Now I work to make impact without pomp. I have found simplicity and brevity are harder.

The tendency to be verbose can come from other roots. Many industry and business experts are so familiar with their own jargon, they cannot see how thick and impenetrable it is to the listener. Professorial trivia buffs have trouble with arcane references that create separation and leave folks behind (seen any Dennis Miller lately?).

Does this mean that we should shy away from using colorful or interesting words? *Au contraire*! But, we must be sure our selections are mindful, and strive to elevate the message, not ourselves.

Each of us has some verbal shortcomings and big words may not be your issue. You may have trouble putting your thoughts together in a clear way; you may be a twenty- or thirty-something for whom *"like"*, *"you know"* and *"totally"* have infected your delivery; you may have a hard time feeling confidant in front of any size group and find that this internal experience corrupts your ability to speak well. Let's face it, we can all turn *up* the heat on purposeful word choice.

There is work to do. The first task is to reflect.

Step one is external. We must have truth reflected back at us, as in a mirror. Seek feedback on your presentations through video, coaching, honest words of colleagues, and evaluations. Now take these numerous and thorough points of view and see how they reflect your eloquence. Are you hearing "to the point," "articulate," or "really kept my attention?" How many said, "Seemed a bit long" or "couldn't quite follow?"

Step two is internal. Usually a critical mass of data is building around us to help reveal blind spots, and if we are quiet we will begin to notice themes in our own professional flaws. Become a watcher to your own play and try to actually listen to yourself while you speak. This will take some time but soon you will be pulled out of your own presenter trance when your words sound over-the-top, meandering, or dull. You will notice when you drone on during your A to a short Q. Speaking of Q's . . . asking yourself reflection questions can help. "Am I saying exactly what I mean?" "What portions of this presentation don't really add anything relevant?" "What would it look like to be in complete command of this room?"

Step three is eternal. As our presentation careers progress, our word choice becomes more perfect and more natural. Eventually we move from Thermometer to Thermostat. A thermometer constantly checks to see what the room feels like. A thermostat hovers at the right mark by making constant adjustments automatically.

And after all of this reflection; Redesign! Here are a few tips to get you started . . .

Twelve Stops on the Road to Eloquence

Upgrade Your Source: Don't stop at your computer thesaurus. Purchase *The Synonym Finder* by J.I. Rodale and Nancy LaRoche. This juicy tome is the difference between the spatula aisle at Vons and William Sonoma.

Off Your Offspring: Writers fall in love with their own words. But, when it comes to editing, the common thought is, you must "kill your children." Go through your presentations and edit listening for overkill, showing off, and repetition.

WWMAD: What would Maya Angelou do? If I were one of the great masters of clarity blended with poetry, how would I say it?

Practice Makes Perfect: Don't feel strange about rehearsing what you are going to say whether it is to an audience of one, three, or 1,000. Nerves can hijack your eloquence in a heartbeat unless they are tamed by practice. Use this discipline especially when speaking in front of anyone who is particularly intimidating to you or who presses that Daddy/ Big Brother/ Hot-Guy-Who-Rejected-You button.

Go Low: Ladies, be aware of when you are chattering away in your high register. To empathize with the male perspective on this sound, try calling to mind the last time your children were whining. Use your low tones. Then give yourself positive and affirming self-talk to add the confidence to back them up.

Follow Through: You know how to follow through in sports. Do the same in speaking. Once the perfect eloquent words are in your speech infuse them with good full breaths. Let your weight drift forward to the balls of your feet. *Li-i-n-n-nger* slightly on the right consonants and *explo-o-ore* your vowels.

Cut That Out: When striving for eloquence on paper cut out the word "that" whenever you can. It is unnecessary 90 percent of the time.

Write It—Edit It: You have 100 words to make a point to a person. Any more and you venture into the territory I like to call "The Avalanche"—pouring tons and tons of information into their very action-oriented minds. Try this—write out everything you want to say and then edit it down to 100 words. When you read it back you will get the feeling of the brevity and directness that make people listen.

Go Easy on Quotes: If you crave more splash in your words, don't borrow them too liberally to meet this need. Too many quotes in a presentation smacks of amateurishness. They came to hear *you*.

Drop the Cookbook: I love to bake because it is an opportunity for instinct and nuance. A good recipe partway through may be abandoned, like a guidebook that at some point is tossed to the tour-bus floor so one can run off and explore. The point is to improvise a bit—even through content you have already written.

Identify Your Recipe: One more baking analogy and then I'm going to have to go whip up a lemon bundt cake so I can get back to concentrating. There are different flavors of eloquence. Ask yourself, what is your eloquence recipe? A spoon of wisdom? A pinch of sweetness or sarcasm? Just a dash of subtlety?

Warm Up: Why write it if your lips can't say it? The most beautiful words need a warm and flexible vocal instrument to be heard. You can sing scales. You can hum a note, sliding up and down. Don't forget the tongue twisters. My favorite; "She stood on the balcony inimitably mimicking him, hiccupping, and amicably welcoming him in."

Welcome to today's words. "Punked" is a verb and Paris Hilton is a role model. We need every well-spoken syllable we can find. So don't give up the fight. Carrying the torch for moving and relevant language is, as it always has been, up to you, to me, and to the occasional odd guy on a box in a public square.

~ JULIET FUNT
Speaker, Author, Talking on Purpose, Inc., www.JulietFunt.com

✦ ✦ ✦

It isn't until you come to a spiritual understanding of who you are—not necessarily a religious feeling, but deep down, the spirit within—that you can begin to take control.

~ OPRAH WINFREY

AFFIRMATIONS FOR PRESENTERS
Read out loud before your presentation.

I am centered.
I let go of anything that has happened today which does
support me to be my best *now*. I put my ego aside and serve
this audience to the best of my abilities. I remain balanced
and centered and am capable of handling anything.

I am knowledgeable.
I have credibility in this topic and present this message in a way that
is easily understood by all. I am professional and respected.

I am calm.
I give thanks that my thoughts flow easily and effortlessly.
My words flow smoothly and in a logical manner. I am safe.
I am confident. I visualize success.

I am connected.
I easily establish and hold rapport with my audience.
I am connected with my audience and shift to respond with them.
I create ways to involve the audience. I empower interaction among
and with the audience participants.

I am dynamic.
I deliver a dynamic presentation. I am amazing.
I am courageous. I am an outstanding speaker.

I am playful.
I take my material seriously and delivery lightly.
I use my talents. I have fun, and they have fun.

I am thankful.
I am worthy to deliver this message. I am grateful for the privilege to serve them. I give thanks that I meet and exceed expectations of all present. I give thanks that I reach each listener on their level.

~ SHERYL ROUSH
Professional Speaker, Speaking Coach, Sparkle Presentations, Inc.
www.SparklePresentations.com
© 2008 Sheryl L. Roush

✦ ✦ ✦

Challenges make you discover things about yourself that you never really knew.
~ CICELY TYSON

Your opinion of me is none of my business.
~ REVEREND TERRI-COLE WHITTAKER

What God intended for you goes far beyond anything you can imagine.
~ OPRAH WINFREY

FOUR KEYS TO AUTHENTICITY

1. Be clear and up-front about your purpose. Let people know about your goals and your mission.
2. Listen to your clients, to your peers, to your friends, and to strangers. Our society has quit taking the time to listen. We are programmed to accommodate X messages per day. With technology and media we are exposed to 100 times the number of messages we can assess, so we shut down. Regular communication is affected by this shut down. We must listen when people attempt to communicate and then respond accordingly.
3. Respond, when someone tells you something, make it a conversation! Let him or her know that you heard and offer feedback, advice, and or a simple note of gratitude.
4. Keep the conversation going. Find a connection or common denominator and continue the conversation. Share resources or experiences and keep the door open for future conversations.

When you follow these four keys to authenticity, you will stay motivated and passionate, and your work will be easy! And that is the power of authenticity!

~ MARYPAT KAVANAGH
Queen of Connections!, Strategic Results Marketing LLC
www.QueenofMarketing.com

THE BEST THINGS ABOUT
A JOB SEARCH

*J*ob hunting is usually not something we look forward to; instead we tend to think of it as an overwhelming necessary evil to be avoided. Hmmm . . . maybe that's why so many people stay in jobs they don't like. In my work as a career coach, helping individuals make job transitions to more fulfilling work, the task of hunting for a job can become the biggest obstacle. I propose we all change our attitude about this and look into this cloud's silver lining to see what opportunities are there:

Change direction: Now's a great time to reassess and see if you want to stay in the same field. Take stock of what you liked best about your last position—was it the environment, the people, the commute? Was it the tasks you performed and the challenges you got to tackle? Chances are, those things can be found in other workplaces regardless of industry. Determine your strengths and favorites and look to other options where they can be found.

Build your network: Networking is hands-down one of the best job search strategies out there. Make a point of visiting an association meeting each week and talking to someone new about your job search every other day. Always end your conversation with "Who else do you know that I can talk to?" Your network should be ever-growing and cultivated regularly for support you'll need at any point in your career.

Personal growth: Here's a good opportunity to stretch and change. "If you always do what you've always done, you'll always get what you've always got" is a great reminder for job searchers. Do something a little different this time—decide what your "dream job" would be and take steps to go after that; take a class and hone a skill you've always been interested in and add it to your resume; track your weekly progress and note your accomplishments.

Set goals and follow action plans: Sharpen your pencil and write down what you can realistically achieve in a week's time. How many resumes and letters will you send? How many phone calls will you make? How many friends and associates will you reach out to? How much time will you spend on the Internet job boards, networking, and making phone calls? Now put an action plan together outlining how you'll accomplish these goals. Then celebrate your accomplishments.

Revisit and revise your resume: Yes, we should all have our resumes ready to go at a moment's notice, working or not, but that usually isn't the case. Take this time to dust off that document, look at it with fresh eyes, gather some resume books or search the Internet for samples, and give it a new look. Then, have someone who's qualified proofread it and give his or her honest opinion on whether or not it will get you in the door for an interview.

Polish yourself up: Take inventory of your closet. Are your shoes and suits in need of minor repairs? Are you about due for a new conservative business outfit anyway? Wear things that are professional and cast the image you want to convey, while being comfortable and showcasing your confidence. Test your handshake, project your voice, smile, and head for those interviews with the look of someone they'd be silly not to hire.

Research: Spend time at the computer looking into local area companies and their websites and decide if that's really where you want to work. Surf a little and find links that take you to related companies and industries you might not have thought of before. Learn all you can about an organization before you enter their door for your interview.

Pump up your attitude: When HR professionals are asked what trait they most look for in candidates, they say enthusiasm! Another can overshadow even someone with all the skills and background with more enthusiasm and fewer qualifications. Show how much you want that job. Be interested and engaged; ask questions of the interviewer, especially, "What's the next step in your decision process?" No matter if this is your first interview with your first choice company or your eleventh interview with the eleventh company on your list—keep showing your enthusiasm. It does pay off. That job you want is just around the corner.

What an opportunity! Your job search can be valuable in so many ways, rather than something to dread. Of course the ultimate goal is fulfilling, steady work with a good income, but job search is that step we all find ourselves in at one time or another. Make the most of it—stretch outside of your comfort zone and make it as enjoyable an experience as possible. See what a little change in attitude can do for you and your career!

~ DEBBIE LOUSBERG
Career Coach and Trainer, www.SmartCareerMoves.net
From Phoenix New Times Help Wanted Magazine *and www.CaliforniaJobNetwork.com*

HOW TO FIRE SOMEONE

I'm not an expert in employment law, so consult your legal and HR people for that important side of your strategy.

*I*s firing someone easy? Oprah, someone I admire, commented in a workshop led by career strategist Marcus Buckingham, "The first time I had to fire somebody, it took me two hours, and at the end of it they said 'You mean I'm fired?' I wasn't very good at it."

My first experience was different. I was nineteen and an office manager. I knew someone I had not hired was doing a terrible job. She had a difficult time understanding even the simplest instructions. She was sweet, but highly ineffective, and after working with her for a reasonable time I had a respectful, cordial meeting with her to tell her it wasn't working out and that I was letting her go.

My move made perfect sense from a functional perspective. At nineteen I wasn't aware of a larger political environment. The president's secretary took me aside and told me the president of our organization had brought in the woman, and that this was a significant factor. After I sweated it out for a couple of days, the woman I'd fired stopped by the office to show us her new engagement ring, and to tell us she didn't have to work anymore. So everyone was happy.

What happens to us when we think about firing someone? It probably brings up old issues. We carry the results of our past conditioning about wanting to please everyone, wanting someone else to take responsibility for important decisions, or just plain not having any role models to help us navigate new human relationship waters. This all plays into our ability to see clearly what we need, and affects our ability to effectively and respectfully handle new human interactions.

We've all been on both sides of "ending a relationship." How comfortable are we initiating change? How do we like to be treated when we're on the receiving end of a request for change?

If we want to cancel a magazine subscription, we're clear about what to do. We call our existing provider and make a clear request, "I want to cancel my subscription," or we return the invoice with a "please cancel" note instead of our payment. If we don't make our wishes crystal clear, nothing will change.

If we want to end a romantic relationship, more of our past conditioning comes into play. We've all probably had more experience ending romantic relationships than firing employees, so let's look at how we've handled those situations.

The most painful breakups for me have been the ones where the guy didn't tell me what he needed because he "didn't want to hurt me." In a work setting, you would probably see a change in the employee's dedication to the quality of their work, their attendance record, or their attitude toward you or others.

One guy stopped returning phone calls, started flirting with other women, broke our dates and was too busy to get together with me. In a work setting, this might look like employee theft, political ill will, and teams not functioning because one is undermining another's efforts. Why treat others disrespectfully? Why not create a safe environment where people can just ask for what they want, and teach communication methods that help people express what they need, and helps others listen?

The breakup I learned the most from involved a triangle. He and I had been dating a while, and suddenly I had a feeling something had changed between us. I asked him about this, and he kept telling me it was my problem, but things just didn't feel right. I felt a painful gap in our connection. I was frustrated with conflicting messages and there didn't seem to be anything I could do to get to the truth.

I happened to know the woman he was involved with before me, and I had respect for her, so I bravely gave her a call. She was wonderful. She told me that the two of them had gotten back together. Then she asked me how I was. She was sincerely interested in my well-being, and kept asking and being attentive to my feelings and needs until I felt supported and connected again.

So I ended up feeling betrayed by the man who professed to care so much about me, and totally supported by the "other woman." Who would I choose to be my friend in the future? The one who told me the truth and then was there to help me heal.

I learned not to assume someone was my enemy. I learned that hearing the truth honestly allowed me to stay connected, and that being treated with respect and being included in the conversation were more important to me than getting my way. The truth allowed me to honestly understand the landscape I was in, so I had more power to chart a meaningful future course of my own.

In a work setting, this might look like not assuming the person you find the most threatening is actually someone to fight with or ignore. If you get to know them, you may find many shared ideas or motivations. Collaborations between people with diverse viewpoints can be very powerful and effective. Maybe your strategy of "getting rid of the irritant" will also deprive you of some important ideas that could lead to innovations in your industry.

You know it's time for you as the leader to step in and do something about an employee that's not working out. This isn't your favorite thing. Where do you start? I say first take your time to get real clear with yourself. What is it that you really need and want from that person or role right now? Try to go a little deeper with your own understanding of yourself, because that will help you get what you need in the process. Make a list of specific behaviors so the person knows exactly what they're doing right, and where things aren't going so well from your perspective.

Then be willing to learn something new from this offending employee whom you are probably pretty frustrated with by now. Acknowledge your feelings to yourself and leave them and your judgments at the door so you can have an honest conversation with this employee.

Listen with sincere interest as the other person (if they feel safe enough with you), reveals what's going on for them. If the words you hear push your buttons, take a deep breath and remember it's not about you; they're just expressing their needs in the best way their skills allow. They're just talking about themselves. If you're interested in developing the person, why not be interested in what's unique about this person?

Then decide together your next step. Consider being creative. You're the captain steering the boat; allow them to inform your decision because respect and trust can build long-term commitment and job satisfaction, or perhaps an advocate if leaving is the best course.

Do we really need more enemies in our lives? I prefer to create more friends.

~ MARILYN MCLEOD
Leadership Coach, www.CoachMarilyn.com

LOVING OUR DIFFERENCES

On my first day at my first corporate job right out of college, I was the odd woman out. In the mid-seventies, a woman in sales at a company like IBM was unusual, even more so an African American woman. I was different ethnically, economically, and culturally. And as a first-generation corporate employee, I had no role models or mentors among my family and friends to help me.

To illustrate how wide the gap was between my colleagues and my parents, not only did they not have college degrees, they were raised in Arkansas as sharecroppers. Rather than the typical summer internship at "my daddy's company," my summer job had been to get on the back of a truck at 4:00 A.M. on the way to pick cotton all day.

I've adjusted to my colleagues since then, but I can't forget the old adage: "The more things change the more they stay the same." As much as today's workers would like to think everything's "A-OK" when it comes to working with people who are different, they still often have difficulty adapting. This truth is becoming more apparent in our increasingly global society. We must recognize that the burden falls on us to create harmony in our own lives by getting along with others. The reality is that we have no choice but to work together; we live in a world where we either provide products and services to people of different cultures or we purchase products and services from them.

It's imperative that we foster a spirit of curiosity so we'll be motivated to understand the cultural basis of people's behavior. In turn, having greater understanding will lead us to successfully interact with those whose backgrounds may be different—often subtly, sometimes radically—from our own.

How many times have you seen someone from a different culture do something, and you didn't know what it meant? Have you noticed that Asian families go shopping together, even when purchasing for only one family member? Many Asian cultures value group effort and decision-making based on consensus. And what American hasn't observed a person with limited English speak "too softly"? It's almost a cultural cliché that in response Americans speak loudly, as if the person is hard-of-hearing rather than merely foreign-born.

In fact, in order to know how to best deal with people who are different from us, it's important to understand, according to psychologist Geert Hofstede, that cultural values are clustered into four areas: **Relationships**, **Activities**, **Time**, and **Environment**.

The dimension of **Relationships** is defined as "the way people within a culture organize their social systems and connect with one another." One culture may see work as a place to make contributions to a group effort, whereas another sees work as a place to be recognized for achievements and for career advancement. In communications, the Western cultural view is that not only is it acceptable to argue, but to do so is "impersonal" because it's about the point or principle. In Asian cultures, such arguments are seen as impolite or as a personal attack, so it's better to just stay quiet.

I once scheduled an appointment with a colleague from the Middle East. When I called, she asked to call me back in fifteen minutes. I didn't feel like she valued my time. Later she apologized, explaining that a family member had come by, and in her culture it was considered offensive if she didn't make time for her family. I learned that she put a high value on family *relationships*.

The dimension of **Activities** is defined as "the way in which people within a culture view the nature and purpose of human actions." Does a culture value "doing" or "being"? In many African and Asian cultures "being" is valued, meaning that self-expression and personal relationships are important to a person's identity. American culture tends to value "doing"—meaning that taking action and individual accomplishments are important to a person's identity.

The dimension of **Time** is defined as "the way in which people within a culture value the passage of time and organize its use." Many of us have gone to vacation spots such as Jamaica or Hawaii where the locals view time as flexible rather than structured. And in the workplace one culture may value decision-making based on tradition, while another culture bases its decisions on future goals.

The dimension of **Environment** is defined as "the way in which people within a culture relate to the world around them." When people must adapt to new situations, they might operate from the view that destiny and fate are set in stone, or that destiny and fate can be changed.

So, how can you begin to use this knowledge to create greater acceptance and harmony in your professional and social relationships?

- *Reserve your judgment of the little things people do and instead seek to understand people themselves.*
- *Recognize the values beneath cultural behavior. Yse your understanding of cultural differences as a springboard for cooperation rather than allowing differences to become a source of conflict.*
- *Be aware of your "filters," that is, the way your culture affects your point of view and your behavior. Avoid unthinkingly applying your frame of reference to others.*
- *Seek to understand your personal cultural style. Tse that understanding to identify and resolve areas of conflict with others.*

continued on next page

Though I grew up with a great deal of diversity, my cultural sensitivity increased as a result of living and working in South Africa for several years. I quickly became aware of the diverse customs of a country that had numerous tribes and eleven official languages. As a Westerner living in a relationship culture, I found that people could be highly credentialed, but if they didn't take time to develop relationships, the chances of gaining someone's business were slim. I also discovered that I was living with people who wanted to avoid personal conflict. If you asked a person to do something they didn't want to do, they didn't say no, they just never got around to doing it.

What I also realized was that it's honorable to ask people about their cultures. Many Westerners believe it's embarrassing to suggest that someone is "different," but people already know they're different. What they really want is to be respected for those differences.

One of the advantages of respecting differences, of not expecting everyone to be the same, is that we can actually lower our stress levels in the workplace. Other benefits include the ability to gain valuable new perspectives and generate greater innovation. The rubber-meets-the-road advantage, of course, is that by starting with an understanding of the four cultural dimensions as well as by following my simple guidelines for respecting others, you can comfortably work with people who are different from you.

From that jumping-off point you can learn to value the cultures of those around you, whether they're colleagues or clients, and vow to honor the unique aspects of each nation of people. And my hope is that ultimately you'll discover a sense of wonder at the true beauty of human diversity.

~ BETTY LAMARR
Executive Coach, www.nadisa.com
© 2008 Betty LaMarr

DIVERSITY

When I was a teenager, a popular sci-fi television show opened with a person receiving the last stages of cosmetic surgery. You heard the doctors and nurses discussing the patient in hushed whispers. The camera focused on the patient's bandaged face. The doctor approached the patient and we saw his white hospital garb rather than his face, as if we were looking from the level of the patient. The inference was the patient had been quite homely and they were hoping the facial surgery would fix the problem.

We observed the hands of the doctor removing the last piece of gauze. Then a surgical instrument clanked to the floor and nurses screamed out at the seemingly grotesque facial features of the patient, who apparently failed his surgery. The camera showed us that he looked normal and handsome. Then it quickly moved up to show us the hospital staff's features—they all resembled pigs.

This memory has stuck with me, as it demonstrates the idea of beauty as being in the eye of the beholder. As long as we can remind ourselves that we're not better, we're simply different, that our ideas are not always right or the best, we can hold a community consciousness that welcomes the input of others.

Co-workers will naturally gravitate to you and want to work with you because they will feel you see their "beauty"—their contribution. They will feel comforted in your presence because you actively listen and respect them. You don't assume, you ask questions and you educate yourself against the stereotyped conclusions of people and situations. You may enjoy similarities, but you don't expect them. You learn from those who are different. Diversity isn't a threat, but a gift.

~ LAURIE SHEPPARD, MCC
Life Coach, Career Strategist, Creating At Will®, www.CreatingAtWill.com

KEY YOUR PAPERS MOVING!

*D*isorganization with your paperwork undermines your creative potential. You can accomplish great things in less time when you are organized. Take a good look at the papers currently in your office.

Are all of your papers in process organized by task and located within arms reach of your workstation or are they spread throughout your office and home? Did you know that according to the *Wall Street Journal*, the average U.S. executive wastes six weeks per year searching for missing information in messy desks and files? I don't know about you, but I would rather spend six weeks every year on vacation than searching frantically for the papers that I need to finish my project!

If you have a home-based office, make sure that your business papers remain in your office. Do not let them encroach into your personal space.

Spend the time to develop a paper flow system. This is as simple as determining what type of action each piece of paper requires in order for it to leave your desktop and creating a holding area for each action step. Finding papers in vertical holders is always easier than in horizontal holding zones. Actions for each piece of paper might include:

- *Calls To Make*
- *Bills To Pay*
- *Waiting For Response*
- *Current Projects*
- *Data Entry*
- *Coupons / Certificates*
- *Upcoming Events*

- *Meetings, To Discuss*
- *Outbound To Others*

Keep your papers in action moving within these categories. This will be one of the most powerful practices you can do to increase your productivity and spend more time doing the things you love.

~ KATHI BURNS
Author, Certified Professional Organizer and Image Consultant
www.AddSpaceToYourLife.com
Excerpt from How to Master Your Muck

✦ ✦ ✦

THE 7 PS

When I joined the family flooring business in 1977, my brother Bob was my teacher and mentor. I learned the ropes, so to speak, from him and am still in the flooring business thirty years later. One valuable piece of advice he gave me was to always remember the 7 P's. In doing so I have succeeded in many facets of this business from sales, warehousing, managing, supervising, and purchasing.

Prior Proper Planning Prevents Pitiful Poor Performance!

Thanks, Bob! You've helped me be the success I am!

~ BECKY PALMER
Creative Touch Interiors, www.ctihome.com

STRESS MANAGEMENT AT WORK

*B*enjamin Franklin once said, " In this world nothing is certain but death and taxes." With apologies to Mr. Franklin, he forgot to include stress. All people feel stress at some time during their life. Often, we see it as a bad thing. We commonly see our stress caused by a host of irritating hassles over a period of time, or an ongoing, difficult situation. Stress affects different people in different ways. Something that causes you a great deal of stress may not affect your friend or coworker in the same way.

Job stress is much like any other form of stress, but can often be more difficult to deal with because we are very aware of being on display at our jobs. We are under pressure to look and act professionally. If you have handled stress at home in ways you would not comfortably handle stress while at work, then you may have also lost your coping mechanism. This, in itself may cause more stress.

What causes stress at work?

Control—I once was a team leader in a group home for disabled adults. I loved my clients and the people I worked with, but I, and many of the other team leaders did not feel supported by the supervisors or our employer. We felt that we had a great deal of responsibility but little control or decision-making authority. This placed us at greater risk of stress and burnout. Individuals in this situation can often develop medical problems due to chronic stress.

Increased responsibilities—Unexpectedly, my employer laid off half of the team leaders at the various group homes and arranged for those remaining to each take responsibility for two residences instead of just one. I had just been given double the workload. I had no choice but to accept the new duties. Increased responsibility can also be difficult for those of us who have problems saying no to added duties. If this sounds like you, it is important to work on how to say no without feeling guilty.

Competence—With my increased workload and greater stress level, I began to doubt my competency to do my job. I also was insecure about my future with my employer. If they could lay off so many people, could they not also get rid of me? Job security and feelings of lack of competence are major sources of stress for many people.

Clarity—An important source of stress for me was the lack of clarity in my job. With the change in the organizational structure, my duties would change wildly from day to day. There seemed to be little purpose or structure in the company. Rather than formulate a plan or goal and stick with it, the organization seemed to follow whatever belief system was popular. A rudderless ship is a stressed ship.

Communication—Do you enjoy going to work every day? Do you know what is going on in your department or the company as a whole? If there is poor communication and you do not feel that you can express your concerns, and more importantly, feel listened to, then you will experience stress. Communication was nonexistent with my employer.

Support—When my father passed away, instead of a supportive environment at work, my employer behaved as if my father's death was very inconvenient for them. I was given three days off, and then I was expected to return to work and perform my job as normal. I felt unsupported and unvalued. The stress I felt was making it more and more difficult for me to feel satisfied in my job.

Significance—With the lack of acknowledgement from my employer, for the work I did, it became more and more difficult to take pride in my work or to find it meaningful. I hated going in to work every day. I was under such great stress that I was becoming ill. For my own peace of mind and for my health, I decided to quit my job.

Later, I discovered that major sources of stress such as the ones above often lead to burnout. Employees can become unhappy and less productive in their work. Job stress can affect your home life as well. While low levels of stress such as a jammed photocopier may not be noticeable, and slightly higher levels of stress can be positive, challenging you to act in a creative and resourceful way, high levels of stress are harmful and can lead to chronic disease.

What can you do about stress at work?
Talk to your supervisor. If you have a performance evaluation on a regular basis, use the time to clear up issues. However, if the issue is pressing, don't wait. Arrange to talk to your supervisor as soon as possible. Don't leave it up to others to begin a dialogue.

Manage your time well. Sometimes, issues between you and your boss, may actually be your fault. Be solutions-focused. Leave your job at the office so you have some time to relax on your time off.

Unplug. You don't have to be available to your office 24/7. That is a recipe for stress. Turn off your cell phone, BlackBerry® and laptop.

Voicemail and e-mail are available so you won't miss anything. Make the technology serve you. Don't become a slave to it.

Know when to quit. If you are completely miserable at your job, and the above suggestions haven't helped, maybe it's time to change jobs. Research other similar jobs, or even a job you have never tried before. It is surprising how many skills are transferable between seemingly unrelated careers. Who knows, you may find that leaving that lousy job was the best decision you ever made.

Stress is a fact of life for most people. While you may not be able to get rid of stress, you can look for ways to lower it. Practice a work/life balance to maintain a healthier lifestyle and to reduce stress.

See which of these ideas work for you:
Exercise. Regular exercise is one of the best ways to manage stress. Walking is a great way to get started.

Write. It can really help to write about the things that are bothering you.

Change negative thinking to positive thinking. It's possible that the other driver did not mean to cut you off in traffic. Give them the benefit of the doubt.

Do something you enjoy. A hobby can help you relax. Volunteer for a charity or do work that helps others. Feeling a sense of accomplishment can be a great stress reliever.

Learn ways to relax your body. This can include breathing exercises, muscle relaxation exercises, massage, aromatherapy, yoga, or relaxing exercises like tai chi.

Practice "being in the moment." Use meditation, imagery exercises, or self-hypnosis. Listen to relaxing music. Look for the humor in life. Laughter really can be the best medicine.

~ PATRICIA STEWART
Co-author of Stress, It's All In The Mind *with Cliff Simon, www.AurorisEntertainment.com*

To keep your communication positive, avoid the following three categories of negative words:

- *Obviously negative words (don't, can't, won't, not, no)*
- *Words with negative meanings (reject, failure, mistake, limit, hesitate, doubt, complain)*
- *Double meaning or potentially confusing negatives (don't know nothing, in all cases except one).*

~ KATHLEEN HAWKINS
Author of Spirit Incorporated: How to Follow Your Spiritual Path from 9 to 5

TIME MANAGEMENT:
THE GREAT WALL OF TIME

Clients who try to crowd their many to-do items onto one line in their tiny electronic calendars or fill their small, hardcopy calendar squares with action steps, are unrealistic. They can't imagine how to fit their goals into their week. I've always coached clients who feel restricted or overwhelmed by space limitations to write their goals on a large wall timeline.

Get a large piece of butcher paper (or tape six 8½" × 11" pages together) and pin it to a wall. Then create what Tim Hurson in *Think Better* calls such a time grid, "The Great Wall of Time." The header on this large page should be labeled time periods from days to weeks to months, a month at a time, or however it's easiest for you to visualize and plan your objective's timeframe.

It's an amazingly simple process, yet immediately feels less restrictive. To make it even more playful, consider using colored crayons or markers. You can underline or highlight the main steps underneath the time periods with your sub-action steps below each of these main steps.

There's no reason that converting your goals into your timeframe as action steps should be a painful, laborious process. It should, however, be clear, complete, and narrowed down to those key steps you are committing to take action on. Surprisingly it can also be fun!

~ LAURIE SHEPPARD, MCC
Life Coach, Career Strategist, Creating At Will®, www.CreatingAtWill.com

Committing to Excellence

A GIFT OF PRAISE

I will never forget a nurse with whom I worked in the operating room when I was in my Obstetrics and Gynecology residency-training program. She was the most competent nurse with whom I had worked. She was also the meanest person with whom I had ever worked. She would as soon chew you up and spit you out, as she would instruct you in procedures. She was especially mean to the medical students who often did not know any better.

The scrubbing and gowning before surgery requires a very specific process so that you are wrapped from shoulder to below the knee in sterile clothing and gloves. It isn't easy to do that and not touch something you shouldn't. If you *do* touch something, then you are contaminated and must start all over again! She had an eagle eye on each of us making sure we did it right. She was looking out for the patient. We didn't want to create any infections either!

It was her attitude that always bothered me, so much so that it occurred to me to ask about her background to verify a suspicion of mine. I told her she always impressed me with her knowledge, preparedness, ability to anticipate the next step, and creativity at the operating room table. Then I asked her if she had ever considered going to medical school, as I felt she would have been very successful.

She said, "Yes, but I married young and had children and couldn't see how I could complete the requirements to become a doctor."

From that day forward, she never was mean to me again. All it took was an acknowledgement of her superb talents and a moment to vent her sorrow about not having been able to use those talents to achieve her dream. I was once again grateful that I had found a way to fulfill mine.

~ CAROL GRABOWSKI, M.D.

COMMIT TO EXCELLENCE

*"I grew disillusioned by midyear and was ready to quit. Mom, however, was determined to see me continue. She insisted, "When you obligate yourself to do a job, you must do your best and finish the task.""**

*T*his advice was given to me when I was sixteen years old and teaching in a rural one-room school in Nebraska. It has been my mantra throughout my thirty-three-year career in federal service from my first job as a bookkeeping machine operator (GS-4 to my position as a manager (GS-15).

It inspired my theme, "Commit to Excellence," when I served as president of Toastmasters International. Jeff Young, the winner of the World Championship of Public Speaking at the 1980 International Convention, expressed it so well in his speech "To Stand Before Kings." His message was that the stature of a person should not be measured by what they do, but how well they do it.

So no matter where you are in the business world, no matter what your job or position, always remember that excellence has no limitation.

~ HELEN BLANCHARD, DTM
First Woman President of Toastmasters International
Author of Breaking the Ice, www.HelenBlanchard.com
© 2008 Helen Blanchard
Excerpt from Breaking the Ice—The Story of the First Woman President of
Toastmasters International

Cultivating a Refreshing Environment

"Promise me you'll paint that wall!" the incoming councilman urged. "You don't like my red wall?" John R. Calhoun, former city attorney, chuckled, feigning surprise.

The truth is, probably only the builder and architect liked the early 1970s red wall. In a plaintiff firm's office it would have inspired confidence. However, in this office it produced anxiety in most human beings the minute they entered the reception area. It was wide, north to south, and tall, east to west.

Flora's own office had a red wall, too, however, not as tall or wide. "This office needs a transformation," Flora thought. She wanted—*needed*—something that was uplifting and soothing to her mental health. And that of others. Flora's positive outlook needed a wall covering that was nourishing and nurturing. However, budget approvals take a lot of time in government offices cloaked with red tape. She didn't wait for the churning wheels of city hall.

"What can transform my own office wall from anxiety producing to soothing?" she wondered. "Temporarily . . . since it's government property." Paint cans were considered. Poster board paints were evaluated. Wallpaper was analyzed. Finally, Flora rifled through her closet. "Ahhhhh," she thought, "this will work nicely." Yards of dusty-rose pink fabric flowed over her arms as Flora turned from the closet.

Carefully, she pressed it flat and crisp with a hot iron, folded it over a hanger, covered it with a dry cleaner's protective bag and hung it in the car. The following day at the office was another normal day, however, Flora stayed very late that evening. She was conspiring with the Universe to calm and nurture people. Quietly, she placed her bag of tricks on the desktop. Out came the fabric. The glue gun and steam iron followed it, then dressmaker pins, clips, tape, staples, a tap hammer, and small nails—just in case.

When the iron was hot, she expertly pressed out the hanger creases. Starting at the top of the wall, Flora gripped the glue gun firmly in one hand and the freshly pressed fabric in the other. "This is it," she thought. Thwack! The glue gun laid down a nice line of hot stickiness. Gently, Flora placed the folded top corner of fabric in just the right spot. Elated that it worked so well, she continued to glue and place fabric until she was done with the wall. Standing back, Flora assessed her work. Iron in hand, she reached high to get a small crease smoothed. "What a difference this makes!" she thought to herself. "Woweeee!"

Coworkers flowed through her office, exclaiming about the difference the missing red wall made. Flora beamed happily, and contentedly. Her office was the place where coworkers and guests came to rejuvenate and refresh themselves. It stopped 99 percent of everyone who went by for the first time.

"H-m-m-m, that plant will look great here," she considered one day. The plant was another victim of a coworker's brown thumb. Flora rescued it too, and placed it to flourish with a handful of others in her nurturing and uplifting office. Classical music played softly in the background; and inspirational messages happily graced the walls and desktop. Discarded plants now thrived on bookshelves. The space was filled with warm, incandescent lighting spilling from a tabletop lamp. The sputtering four-cup coffee pot brought plenty of foot-traffic to her doorway, smiling about the fragrance of fresh brew wafting in the hallways.

Flora's office lovingly fed many of the five senses of those who came to the eleventh floor in city hall. Her colleagues and coworkers often "borrowed" her ideas to use for cultivating their own refreshing workspace. It fed Flora too, and she delighted in her work and the people around her.

~ BELINDA SANDERS
Freelance Writer, www.BelindaSandersConsulting.com
© 2008 Belinda Sanders

❖ ❖ ❖

Find a purpose you are crazy about and go nuts! Southwest Airlines Employees are often accused of being nuts—when in fact all we are is celebrating life. We celebrate each other. We celebrate our Customers. And we celebrate being different!

~ LIDIA MARTINEZ
Manager, Corporate Community Affairs, Southwest Airlines Co.

The secret of joy in work is contained in one word—excellence. To know how to do something well is to enjoy it.

~ PEARL S. BUCK
Author

If you give your life as a wholehearted response to love, then love will wholeheartedly respond to you. Love is the intuitive knowledge of our hearts.

~ MARIANNE WILLIAMSON
Author of A Return to Love

September Days

In September I still get a twinge,
Watching them trudge along under the burden of backpacks,
Toes stuffed in sneakers, longing for the freedom of flip-flops.
I miss the fresh scrubbed faces and the smudged ones, too.
I miss the high-pitched squeals at recess
and the muffled voices at "quiet time."
But most of all I miss the open minds,
Waiting to be filled with numbers and letters
and all the wonders of First Grade.
And I worry that those beautiful minds will close,
Numbed by tests and homework,
Mesmerized by electronic devices.
I am saddened by the longing and the loss.

~ JANICE WEIGHT
Retired Teacher

✦ ✦ ✦

Success means we go to sleep at night knowing that our talents and abilities were used in a way that served others. We're compensated by grateful looks in people's eyes, by whatever material abundance supports us in performing joyfully and at high energy, and by the magnificent feeling that we did our bit today to save the world.

~ MARIANNE WILLIAMSON
Author of A Return to Love

The Boss's Daughter

Seven years after leaving high school and floundering around trying to decide my course in life, I joined the family floor covering business. How proud I was to be part of Hal Palmer's Carpets and Interiors! The boss (my dad Hal), had me working in all aspects of the business, from the warehouse to paper pusher to sales. I learned from the ground up! For the most part he treated me like the other employees—no favoritism here. In fact I had to go that extra step to prove I was capable of any task he gave me.

There were mixed reactions from customers and vendors when they found out that I was related. Some thought I had it easy, (little did they know I had to work twice as hard), some sales reps glossed over the fact that I might know something in favor of the "higher-ups," and there were always side comments from other employees.

Mostly I shined it on, learned to toughen up my skin and not let it bother me what they thought. I felt my actions spoke louder than their suppositions. I learned to lead by example, to excel at communication once I had joined Toastmasters International and to dispel any rumor that I had it easy or was favored. Contrary to belief, I was the last to know major announcements, the last to be told new policy implementations, and the first to be tossed extra work!

I had to crawl out from under the stigma of being "Hal's daughter" and become Becky.

Twenty years later I am still in the flooring business, still leading by example, and practicing effective communication skills. I have finally become Becky and can now look back and appreciate what I went through being the "boss's daughter."

~ BECKY PALMER
Creative Touch Interiors, www.ctihome.com

TRUST YOUR INTUITION

*T*he job interview process is interesting. As a hiring manager, you prepare a job description; place it in the right medium to maximize exposure to candidates, and hope for the best in terms of receiving resumes from strong potential applicants you might eventually call in for an interview.

Scouring through hundreds of respondents is an arduous process. Sometimes there is something undefined about a resume, which strikes you. You know that you must truly stop and take the time to evaluate it. That is the case with the resume of Stephanie Darden.

It was nearly two decades ago, but I can still remember an unlikely sparkle in the resume, the instantaneous realization that I was in possession of a great chronicle. I couldn't dial the phone fast enough to arrange an interview. I knew my intuition was telling me: this candidate was going to be extraordinary.

Stephanie arrived ten minutes to noon, a good sign. I greeted her in the lobby of our suite and escorted her to my office. The first thing I noticed about her was her infectious smile and overt confidence, which again confirmed that my intuition wasn't leading me astray. I had learned, after many years of interviewing candidates, it was dangerous to have a preconceived notion about a candidate, so I remained cautious about the interview. My cautiousness faded to excitement with each of Stephanie responses. It was clear to me, about an hour into the interview, that she was the *one*. I happily pranced down the hallway to the vice president's office.

"Sharon, I have the *one* in my office," I gleefully announced.

"Let me look at her resume," Sharon demanded. After years of working with the VP, I knew timing was everything, and I could sense the timing this day might not work in the candidate's favor.

"No, not interested," Sharon scowled decisively. I had been recruiting for weeks to find the perfect candidate to fill her assistant opening, and in five short seconds, she was dismissing the *one*.

"Sharon, trust me, this is the *one*," I appealed. I knew if I were persistent, Sharon would reconsider her initial judgment.

"Okay, ten minutes is all I have," Sharon, announced.

I sprinted down the hallway to my office and clutched Stephanie by the arm. "Let's go, you have only ten minutes to impress."

I'm certain that she must have thought I was insane, as the look on my face registered an unnatural urgency.

Ten minutes evolved into a half an hour which continued to an hour, and that's when Sharon's door swung open, and I could hear her say, "Jan will contact you with the details, when can you start?"

Stephanie worked for Sharon for more than ten years, not an easy accomplishment, as the position was demanding. Stephanie proved herself a highly revered and respected employee to anyone who crossed her path. Sharon and Stephanie grew to respect each other's weaknesses and vulnerabilities, and forged a seemingly lifelong relationship, even though Sharon eventually left the company.

At Stephanie's untimely funeral, I noticed Sharon in the crowd of hundreds. We greeted each other with a sad regret over a life ended too soon. Sharon took me aside and with a distressed voice said, "I'm glad I didn't say no, and I'm glad you forced me to consider hiring Stephanie, and I am appreciative that you trusted your intuition."

Sharon tells me that she still keeps Stephanie's picture on her desk mantle in her office. A gentle reminder there are some things that are unexplainable, like a certain sparkle from a resume.

~ JAN M. SMITH
Inland Management Group, www.inlandmgtgroup.com

Validating Others—
Even When They Don't Like You!

*I*f you have ever worked alongside an angry person, or someone who doesn't like you for any reason, this story will give you some tools and ideas. The important thing to remember is to set your intention, which is hopefully to create a workable situation for the highest and best good of everyone involved.

I was hired by a start-up company to assist the CEO and other corporate officers, as well take on the HR manager responsibilities. During the interview process, I was told I was replacing another employee whom I will call "Violet." Upon further investigation, I was told Violet was being "let go" because no one liked her—she was just too hard to get along with—she had an angry disposition and intimidated the employees.

My gut reaction when I heard this was "everyone has a positive intention for his or her behavior." I asked if Violet was well educated for her position, how long she had been employed. I learned that she had a master's degree, had been with the company since inception, was very bright, but appeared to only get along with the VP of engineering (a woman with many of the same angry behavioral issues).

When I determined that the company could afford to keep her on payroll, I proposed that there might be a way for Violet to assist the VP of engineering, thereby utilizing her valuable company history, as well giving her an opportunity to grow. I have always inherently believed that everyone has a gift to bring to the table, workplace, or otherwise. I was told by the CEO, a very kind and compassionate man, that I was setting myself up for more problems than it was probably worth. However, he agreed to keep her on as long as she was not interfacing directly with the other employees (mostly engineers), and mandated that she attend anger management classes. I was soon to find out just how angry Violet was!

For the first few months of my employment, Violet took every opportunity to "get in my face," refused to give information I needed to do my own work, and was very angry that I had been brought in to replace her. (Yet, I noticed she did appear to be motivated by her new assignment.) At first I found I was tiptoeing around her to avoid interaction, and becoming stressed myself, as I needed important information from Violet. Also, as HR manager, I had a responsibility to address her very angry outbursts with others. I was at the point of regretting my insistence that she remain employed. Then, I remembered a way of "rapport building" I had learned called "LAMA." This stands for "Listen, Acknowledge, Make a statement, and Ask a question."

One day, I walked into her cube and asked Violet a work question. As usual, she stood up and loomed close to me, her face stretched into ugly proportions, spitting venom with every word! Instead of shrinking back, I decided to take on her physical visage. I squared my shoulders, mirrored her expression to the best of my ability (I surely looked very mean and scary), and using the same hateful tone of voice, I spat out "I know exactly what you mean! If I were you, I would feel exactly the same way you do! I wonder how we are going to work this out?" Then I turned and stomped angrily out of her cube.

Within an hour, Violet was at my desk asking me if I would like to have lunch the next day. I was amazed that, even with my angry expressions, she only heard and responded to the words I had spoken! We met for lunch regularly after that, where I created a safe place for her to unload and share her own frustrations on the job. She was able to share her feelings with me about her life and where she believed her anger was coming from. Over the course of our working relationship, I continued to validate her feelings by *1. listening, 2. acknowledging or validating what I heard, 3. making a statement about it, and 4. asking a question.* What a great learning experience for me!

Because of Violet's anger, I learned to listen to my gut feelings about what was really going on under the surface. I also learned that courage means standing in the face of what I am experiencing at the moment, with confidence in my ability to listen deeply, and to respond for the highest and best good for everyone . . . which can magically change the outcome of any situation.

~ CAROL J. SHIELDS
Realtor, Former HR Professional, www.WineCountryCrush.com

✦ ✦ ✦

Coming together is the beginning, keeping together is progress, working together is success.

~ HENRY FORD

Think of your career as your ministry. Make your work an expression of love in service to mankind.

~ MARIANNE WILLIAMSON
Author of A Return to Love

You know you are on the road to success if you would do your job, and not be paid for it.

~ OPRAH WINFREY

WAITING FOR JUMOKE

I grew up in central Pennsylvania and lived more than 200 miles from the nearest zoo. I had the opportunity to visit the Pittsburgh Zoo only once in my childhood, and the giraffes made a huge impression on me. Their height, their grace, and their eyelashes seemed magical. And they had freckles too, just like me. Fascinated, I read books about them and collected stuffed animals and figurines.

As an adult I am lucky to be a tour guide in the Photo Caravan Department at the San Diego Wild Animal Park. I cannot believe I get to spend time with giraffes every day in my job! Surely during my time here, I would be able to witness something I had always hoped to see—the birth of a baby giraffe. A couple of years later, a giraffe named Chocolati was nearing the end of her pregnancy, but had not been put inside the boma and because she was an experienced mother, they decided to let her have her baby in the field enclosure.

A few days later I came to work and found out that Chocolati was in labor. Maybe today would be the day! Near the end of our second tour, my guests and I watched Chocolati in amazement as we saw hooves emerge. My driver and I went out on the last tour of the day with guests as excited as we were. When we arrived at the East Africa enclosure, we saw that the labor had progressed and the baby's head was now visible. Other female giraffes were attending the birth. We could feel their sense of excitement and community. It was as if they were encouraging her—"You're doing great!" "Just a few more pushes." Chocolati gave a final push and the baby fell to the ground with a splash and a thud. Mom and two attending females pulled off the birth sac together. What an amazing sight! The whole event was better and more emotional than I had imagined.

A keeper drove into the field to check on him and came to tell us that the baby was breathing and we had nothing to worry about. Easy for him to say, I thought. Did he know what I had been through that day? As the sun was setting and the light was fading, we all went home with mother and weak calf in our thoughts and hearts. The next day we drove into the field and there stood this handsome, strong, young male who had been named Jumoke, totally unaware of the drama and joy that had accompanied his arrival.

~ VICKI NOTARO
Wild Animal Park, Zoological Society of San Diego, www.SanDiegoZoo.org

✦ ✦ ✦

The greatest ability in business is to get along with others and influence their actions. A chip on the shoulder is too heavy a piece of baggage to carry through life.
~ JOHN HANCOCK

Our career is an extension of our personality.
~ MARIANNE WILLIAMSON
Author of A Return to Love

You don't get what you deserve. You get what you think you deserve.
~ OPRAH WINFREY

WHEN THE DOOR OPENS

*I*t's a long way from a one-room school on the Kansas prairie with outhouses and a wood stove to a television credit on *Hill Street Blues*. I stepped into the world and used my shortcomings as assets.

My Dad was a goat dairy farmer. The dairy dictated our lives seven days a week. One Sunday, when I was thirteen years old, we took the afternoon off and went fishing on the Four-Mile creek. We laughed and talked and forgot work—what a relief it was from the usual routine. On the way home we drove past a farm that Daddy told us belonged to the internationally famous fire fighter Red Adair. There was no truck in the driveway, so of course I thought, he is out somewhere in the world fighting fires. As we drove on I made a promise to myself that I would not stay in Kansas, I would not be a farmer's wife, in fact, like Red Adair, the world would be my home.

Thirteen years later, when my sons were in elementary school, I went back to college at Wichita State University. I majored in art, knowing that I would find something I could do in that field of study. I am dyslexic and thought college was out of reach for someone who was not a good reader.

Two years later I was taking a painting class and my husband was singing in an opera workshop. After class, I walked to the music building to meet him and ride home. We chatted with the opera director who asked if I could sew. I said "yes," and he asked how well I sewed. I said, "If you show me a picture I can make it." I thought he was talking about an evening gown for his wife. He asked if I thought I could construct an eighteenth century opera. I thought for a moment and remembered that there was a Martha and George Washington Halloween costume in the Simplicity pattern book. A voice in my head said "Do it," so I said, "Yes, I will construct the opera costumes." I was in over my head—I was inventing every step—but it felt like this was the thing I should be doing. The next year, the designer graduated and I was asked to design my first opera, *The Marriage of Figaro*. At that time it didn't occur to me to look at costuming as a potential career.

Nine complete operas and a Bachelor of Fine Arts degree later, I was on my way to the University of Texas at Austin to learn how to do what I had been stumbling through. Professor Emeritus, Lucy Barton, had come to WSU to speak at a costume seminar. She reviewed my design portfolio and commented that I had a lot to learn. She said she thought I would profit from studying with a former student, Dr. Paul Reinhardt, who was the head of the costume department. Once again the voice in my head said, "Do it." Motivational trainers tell us to set goals, write them down, determine the steps to achieve that goal, and set a timetable.

Psychologists describe how the brain identifies a goal and recognizes components of that goal as they pass through your life. I call that quality: "When the door opens—just walk through it." My mind seems to make a quick evaluation of the opportunity and if it is right for me it states the intent to "Do it." Each time I jump in over my head—I am confident because I work with three success qualities: a practical sense of finding solutions, calm determination, and a positive attitude.

While at UT I got the opportunity to design costumes for the PBS show *Carrascolendas*. When I saw my work on camera, I knew that was the medium for me. The camera allows the viewer to be a part of the action. I liked the close-up detail and the challenge of creating characters the viewer could recognize and know their psychology.

Maybe contemporary costuming works with my dyslexic mind. My research is first hand. Wherever I am I watch people. I look at news stories of real people on TV, in the newspaper and magazines. I am looking at pictures; I am inputting visual information, not word information. I have come to call myself a "social psychologist." I observe how people are dressed and watch how they function in their society.

I left behind the grand period costumes and moved into costuming real people—illustrating their stories. I met directors from the PBS and the Hollywood TV worlds during the two years I designed costumes for *Carrascolendas*. Through those connections I met legendary Hollywood costume designer Dorothy Jeakins. I wrote about her work for my MFA thesis at UT. During my three interviews with her, I was privileged to see many of her sketches and discuss the details of her design process. I also interviewed people who had worked with her.

Seven months after *Carrascolendas* was canceled, I turned in my thesis at 4:30 P.M., and by 7 P.M. my son and I were on the road headed west out of Austin with $400 in my pocket, an Exxon credit card and a place to stay in Los Angeles. "The Door Opened and I Walked Through It." I stored the household goods in Austin, just in case, with the idea that I would send for the stuff when I was established. I was in Los Angeles for ten days when I got the opportunity to interview for a position as set costumer on a new show, *Lou Grant*. That was the beginning of my twenty-five-year career in Hollywood. My claim to fame is that my name is on every episode of *Hill Street Blues*. Some of my other credits include *Dear John*, *The 60s* mini series, and the film *Motel Hell*. I ended my career at the conclusion of the first season of *The District* in 2001. There were good days and bad days, but overall I wouldn't trade my career for anything.

My high school debate partner commented recently that perhaps the dyslexia caused me to look a little harder to find a career that suited me better and made me happier with my work than many people are with their work. I found a career that matched how I could work and yet something that challenged me. I have come to know I like to work fast. I like short-term projects. I wanted every day to be different—different locations, different people. I am not afraid of unknown challenges (surprises). Going to the same office every day would not have been a good choice for me. I believe I moved forward to success because I listened to my instinct, I worked hard, conducted business with integrity, and a projected a healthy attitude.

It's a long way from a one-room school in Kansas to a costume credit on *Hill Street Blues*. Bottom Line: "When the Door Opened— I Walked Through It." I hope you do too!

~ KAREN HUDSON
www.KarenHudsonSeminars.com

✦ ✦ ✦

My old friend of 80 years young once remarked about how ironic it is that we complain that our jobs require so much work. Wasn't that what we said we wanted when we applied for the job?

~ CAROL GRABOWSKI, M.D.

Light Moments

Benefit Package

When my husband retired, I worried.
What would occupy his time while I worked on my writing?
He found his digital camera to be his constant companion
and soon his mornings and afternoons were filled
with pictures of flowers, birds and beautiful views of the lake.
Happy and content, he rarely emerged from his
work station: the spare bedroom.

My office doubles as our bedroom.
One afternoon after nearly a month of retirement, he stood
at the doorway to my office and said, "You're a slave driver!"
I shook my head not understanding what he meant.
When I asked, "Why?" he sputtered,
"At my old job, they at least gave us breaks!"

I smiled and agreed but reminded him
that lunch times now are long and laid-back
and *happy hour* comes with good conversation and fine wine.
And as far as his new job is concerned, the pay isn't great
but the benefit package is priceless.

~ MARY LENORE QUIGLEY
Author of Indelible Ink: A Memoir

GREAT DAYS AT WORK

*W*hat makes a day at work a great one? Often the surprises come out of nowhere. I remember when I was working as a bank teller for the summer and a woman stepped up to my window ready to deposit her paycheck and make a withdrawal. She wasn't alone. Her small son was standing beside her, his head barely reaching the counter top. He had to tilt his head back to talk to me. His eyes were as big as saucers as he asked me, "Do you have a hundred dollars there?"

I was glad I was sensitive enough to answer him with a simple, "Ye-e-s, I do!" knowing full well I had about $15,000 in that drawer. Fifteen thousand would have been as irrelevant to him as trillions are to me. I made his day and he made mine!

~ CAROL GRABOWSKI, M.D.

FOREVER FOUR

*W*hen my now-sixteen-year-old daughter was born, it occurred to me that I knew nothing about child rearing. Sure, I had been a working person and supervisor for many years, but my expertise on children was limited. Being a university administrator at that time, I decided to do some research—a one-year subscription to various parenting magazines. One of the juicy nuggets of wisdom frequently shared in these magazines: "By the age of four, your child's personality is formed. That's who he or she is going to be *forever*!"

Yikes! Many intimidating thoughts such as this one jumped from the pages, but I continued to read month after month. A startling realization occurred to me at the end of my one-year subscription: In reading these parenting magazines, I had learned more about how to handle my co-workers than I had about raising my daughter!

Here's an experiment: Next time you walk into the office, you will run into that challenging person—you know, the one whose voice sounds like that of the teacher in the Peanuts cartoons: "Wah wah wah!" When you hear that voice, don't react or let them push your buttons. Instead, just look at the person. In your mind, I'd like you to be thinking: He's been this way since he was four years old!

This was my big wake up call! Who do I think I am that I can go to one seminar or read one book and then try to change this person? How empowering for me to realize that this person has been this way for a very long time! What a relief to decide that it was no longer in my job description to try to change or fix them! When changing and fixing the other person is no longer the goal, this certainly sets the stage for positive communication.

~ SARITA MAYBIN
Speaker, Author, www.SaritaMaybin.com
Excerpt from If You Can't Say Something Nice, What DO You Say?

IN PURSUIT OF
LESS CHALLENGING WORK

They gathered around the large rock that was blocking the only entrance and exit to their place of business. They couldn't dismiss it or go about their business. The cost involved in not eliminating it soon could be substantial for all. They needed to focus on other projects, but this was certainly an imminent concern. Assigning outside workers to this project would take a while for them to be reached and take others away from their work tasks. The costs of assigning workers to a new route could take a long time. They were going to have to find a way to handle it now.

"But wait a minute," someone asked. "How'd the rock get here in the first place?" The inference was that someone was to blame. Another voice was heard, "It wasn't here last week when I came by and whoever knew about this should have handled it sooner." The accusations mounted. "Someone should take the lead on this!" Yet no one spoke up. No one stepped forward.

"Well, I have other priorities for my time," said a harsh voice and a few others nodded in agreement. They moved away, leaving a smaller group staring blankly at the rock.

"We don't have the authority to make any modifications on this route and it'll take too long to get them," said someone in the group. A brave voice added, "It's my understanding that we were assigned to a team project, so it seems it would be up to each of us to be responsible for unexpected outcomes." A guilty silence fell on the group.

"I won't wait any longer," was heard and someone stepped forward and attempted to push away the rock until a small chunk fell off it with a thud to the ground. When it did, it broke into several other smaller pieces.

Cheers rose up in the group. One-by-one they each approached the rock and banged it till it broke into smaller pieces. Those closest to it passed the smaller pieces to others who in turn carried it off the path and away from the entrance to the ant nest.

Though none of them knew how it had fallen in the path of the ant nest, nor did they care at this point, they toiled for several days until they'd removed the large crumb that blocked their route. Their teamwork, cooperation, and trust in each other had created a food source for all of them. It fed them for a great while, while those who had left the group early on, spent their time laboring day and night in pursuit of less challenging work and food gathering that didn't depend on others.

~ LAURIE SHEPPARD, MCC
Life Coach, Career Strategist, Creating At Will®, www.CreatingAtWill.com

✦ ✦ ✦

If I knew then what I know now: I'd be someone else.

~ KRISTEN CRAWFORD
Speaker, Odds On Success

Our childlike self is the deepest level of our being.

~ MARIANNE WILLIAMSON
Author of A Return to Love

New Dress Code

*H*ow many great ideas have you left unsaid, because you couldn't think of a witty remark on the spot? Why not? You were probably nervous, preoccupied, or apprehensive. This is what stress does to us—it keeps us from offering others our best, keeps us from creating an inviting environment, keeps us from having fun.

I had a relaxing day at the massage therapist, and it was a great opportunity to co-create a lot of comedy material. When we're relaxed, we CAN think up clever things, mainly because we are NOT pressured, we are not being graded, and we are not being judged. So we let it all out.

My massage therapist asked me how often I run. I said, "Every day." She said, "You're disgusting! That was my goal at the beginning of the year—" I interrupted, "What—to be disgusting?"

Then we moved on to my interests. I said I can go to the beach, but I get bored after one day, it's enough. "I would rather ice skate." She replied, "Oh, the beach is boring, but going around a circle for an hour and a half isn't?"

It was amazing how easy it was for both of us to ping-pong back and forth, and to recognize the absurdity of each other's remarks. When we are in everyday work situations, we might miss these comedy opportunities because we aren't laying on a table half-naked. Maybe your workplace should get a new dress code?

What have *you* done today to be a comedy catalyst?

~ TRINA HESS
"Cleana Trina" Humorist, www.YourShiningExample.com

Being a single working mother, I had given my daughter advice that she shouldn't call me at work unless it was important. We could talk when I got home. One day the phone rang and it was my daughter asking if she could go to the beach with her friends. I had forgotten that when you are a teenager, going to the beach WAS important.

~ SHIRLIE CUNNINGHAM
Accounting Administrator, AEI-CASC Consulting, Inc.
www.aei-casc.com

I called my mother crying.
"Kristen, what's the matter? Why are you crying?" she said in a panicky voice.
"I-I-I-I think I ma-ma-might get fired from my job!" I sobbed.
"Do you know what you'll be doing if that happens?" she asked, chuckling.
"No. What?" I whimpered.
"You'll be looking for a job just like you were; when you found this one."
It made me fearless.

~ KRISTEN CRAWFORD
Speaker, Odds On Success

Best Practices, Strategies & Ideas

LEADING WITH HEART

*H*istorically, leaders have demonstrated many approaches and unique styles, yet one sincerest commonality—that of heart—passion, zeal, fervor! This is true be it a manager in a corporate environment, volunteering for an organization, position, or title in today's workplace, or a woman who owns her own business. Granted there are gender, cultural, and generational considerations, yet "heart" is still at the core.

Rudy Giuliani, mayor of New York City during the 9/11 crisis, writing in his book *Leadership,* defines these traits of effective leaders: know your values; be hopeful; be prepared; show courage; build great teams; and above all, love people.

The heart of a leader is one that constantly expands to encompass, embrace, and encourage. One who leads with authenticity amazes even themselves at the capacity to exceed their own expectations, limitations, and fortitude. They have core values, solid beliefs, and practiced principles by which they live. That "heart" then shapes the personality, attitude, style of their leadership, and day-to-day actions.

What Do People Want?

As a conference speaker and corporate trainer for twenty years, I have the privilege of getting to know organizations from the inside-out, discovering what makes them tick, and how to help people bring their heart and spirit to their work. I tailor every program, beginning by asking the client questions to enrich my understanding of the organization, its genuine needs, and then I craft their presentation. Often I become an "interpreter" between upper management and those who work for them, bridging the needs gap and bringing teams together, all conveyed with conviction and lightheartedness.

When there is negativity and low morale, people need to feel valued, appreciated, and treated with dignity and respect. When there is stress, overwhelm, and burnout, people need life balance. When there is lack of teamwork, people need to reconnect to the mission and the big picture, working through their differences.

Being assigned "interesting and challenging work" is at the top of the list of what people want. People want to be kept informed on work-related subjects, be recognized for their skills, and empowered to do a job well. People do want to be delegated tasks, but not "dumped on." It is *how* the work is assigned. People want to be given the opportunity to improve their skills, plus the resources needed to do their job. People want their ideas "heard," even if those ideas cannot be implemented. People want to see the end result of their work, and feel good about it, and their contribution. They want to work for efficient and effective managers (which is a skill-building series of seminars by itself).

Are We Having Fun Yet?

Employees and volunteers come to great organizations because of their reputation, affinity, and opportunity to serve, with potential for advancement and challenge. (Okay, some do come for the money.) They embrace centered leadership, support a vision that has significance, and are driven when feeling personally fulfilled by the cause and their contribution to it. They leave because those needs are not being met.

Harvard University psychological theorist David C. McClelland, indicates that there are three things that make a great place:

1. You trust the people with whom you work;
2. You have pride in your work; and
3. You enjoy the people with whom you work.

My personal mission is to help rekindle the spirit and raise the bar, through boosting communication skills, positive attitudes, and fun. Your co-workers (and boss) are like little three and four year olds dressed up in business attire. They want—and need—to have fun too. When people have fun doing their tasks, productivity, problem solving, creativity, and innovation increase; margins of error decrease; deadlines and schedules are met; and morale, teamwork, and cooperation elevate. Having fun DOES affect the bottom-line.

The New Paradigm

Yesterday's masculine leadership style of control, manipulation, and intimidation are old school and ineffective. Today, people are the most valuable asset in any organization, and effective leaders are learning to celebrate and value the skills of individuals on their team, harness intrinsic motivators to make their people shine. Human resource departments are shifting old paradigms to "talent management" to retain quality staff and those valued "human assets." As Steve Forbes declares, "The real source of wealth and capital in this new era is not material things—it is the human mind, the human spirit, the human imagination, and our faith in the future."

Involve Me, Please!

Our lives need to have meaning and significance today, more than ever. Warren Bennis, bestselling author of *Leaders* and *On Becoming a Leader*, concludes that at least 15 percent of an organization's success is due to leadership. Professor Bennis further believes, "Good leaders make people feel that they're at the very heart of things, not at the periphery. Everyone feels that he or she makes a difference to the success of the organization. When that happens people feel centered and that gives their work meaning."

What Does It take?

Leadership, management, and mentorship are siblings in the same family. Our world will always need all three. What does it take to truly be a great leader today? As the song lyrics from Van Buren Benny suggest, "You've 'gotta have heart!"

~ SHERYL ROUSH
Speaker, Sparkle Presentations, Inc., www.SparklePresentations.com
© 2008 Sheryl L. Roush

✦ ✦ ✦

If you work just for money, you'll never make it, but if you love what you're doing and you always put the customer first, success will be yours.

~ RAY KROC
Founder of McDonald's

"Leadership is not so much about technique and methods as it is about opening the heart. Leadership is about inspiration—of oneself and of others. Leadership is not a formula or a program, it is a human activity that comes from the heart and considers the hearts of others. It is an attitude, not a routine."

~ LANCE SECRETAN, PHD
Industry Week

GOAL SETTING:
FIVE STEPS TO STAY ON TRACK
WITH YOUR BUSINESS

To be truly successful when you own a business, it's vital to have a passion for what you're doing and for helping others. We should devote a lot of time to praying about a business *before* we make a decision to start it. And if we take an honest look at our spiritual gifts and the skills that we have developed in our life, we should be able to choose a business that suits us well over the long term. Pay attention to that still small voice and look for the sense of peace that God will give you about a right decision. Here are a few tips on keeping yourself motivated and on track with your business:

Spend time with God. Nothing builds purpose and motivation like time spent praying through concerns and needs and just enjoying His presence.

Spend time with those who are precious to you. Money and success alone are empty for the business owner. It's great to achieve a new level of accomplishment but in the end it's our friends and family that we treasure, not our businesses. So don't let work overpower all of your nights and weekends. As we work hard to provide for our families and to support others is what will help us keep some balance.

Use a daily list. By taking large projects and breaking them down into smaller bite size activities for your daily plan it not only makes those large projects easier to handle, it helps you manage your time.

~ REGINA BAKER, COO
e-commerce Solutions for Small Businesses, www.Wahmcart.com

ELEVEN TIPS TO BRING YOUR GOALS *ALIVE*

*D*id you begin the year ready to CREATE? How many of your New Year resolutions have you kept? The following tips, from a confessed goal junkie, are highlights from more than 20 years of motivating employees, clients, and herself to achieve goals:

Value them. They must be in alignment with what you personally value most NOW or you will not be motivated to pursue them.

Allow them to challenge you. They must cause you to stretch and climb out of your comfort zone. When you feel a little uncomfortable that is a good sign!

Be flexible. Remember that your goals are not made of cement. Life happens and sometimes you may need to shift course. If that happens, be gentle with yourself and make a course correction. If you find yourself avoiding a goal, it is okay to ask, "Is this what I really want?" If it isn't, give yourself permission to scratch it off the list and move on to what you really want.

Own them. Your goals are exactly that—yours. Do not make them the property of your family members or friends. Make sure they are yours. Ask, "Whom am I doing this for?"

Pace yourself. Achieving a goal is like running a marathon. It is *not* a series of 100-yard sprints. If you approach them in that way, you will wear yourself out. Be gentle and patient with your progress. Accomplish it bit by bit and you *can* achieve it. An anonymous quote I once read sums it up well, "Yard by yard life is hard, inch by inch it's a cinch!"

Be discreet. Be careful with whom you share your precious dreams and goals with. Naysayers will drag you down. Negative people and pessimistic thoughts will drain your energy. Surround yourself with positive people. Only share your dreams and goals with those you know you can trust.

Protect your energy. Watch your self-talk and keep it positive. Fill your mind with encouraging words. Whenever you can, read uplifting materials and affirmations. Every time you make a decision ask, "Does it take me closer to or further from my goal?" (You might add, "Is it giving me or taking my energy?) And there is your answer!

Reach out for support. Build your own support system. If you really want your goals, yet feel afraid, ask, "Whom can I turn to or what can I do to support myself in taking a step toward this goal?" Call a close friend or family member who understands and will listen. Find a support group. Hire a life and/or business coach to encourage and guide you. The hand that reaches out will *always* be grasped by another. TRUST! If the fear of failure or rejection ever nudges you, reassure yourself with this beautiful message from nature:

> *Use the talents you possess, the woods would be very*
> *silent if no birds sang there except those that sang best.*
> —Henry Van Dyke

Remember that birds that sing best have spent years practicing!

Persist. It is your determination that achieves your goals—more than your talents! Review your goals daily (each morning when you wake up and each evening before you go to bed). Visualize the completed goal(s). Take the action(s) step by step. Imagine a 500-pound marshmallow stands in your way—eat it bite by bite—otherwise it is too much of a challenge to swallow. Ask, "What am I waiting for?" Remind yourself that this isn't a dress rehearsal. This *is* life. What are you waiting for?

Stay focused. Be aware of the distractions that want to steer you off course. Have a plan to distract your "attraction to distraction." Then work your plan each day. Consider eliminating things from your life to create more space for your goals to flourish and then take action. For example, let's imagine that your distraction is watching television. The hours you expend watching the tube could instead be spent creating what you want.) "What is it for YOU? How willing are you to have what you really want for your life?

Reward yourself. When you complete a goal—reward yourself with a treat such as scheduling a massage, dinner out with a friend, or buying concert tickets of your favorite group. Sing your own praises. Let everyone know! (Now you can have chats with the naysayers). You deserve this recognition. Release the tendency to rush on to the "next thing." Take the time to acknowledge your accomplishments. Bask in the radiance of *pure joy.*

~ SUZAN TUSSON, CPCC
Author, Award-winning Author and Certified Life Coach, http://wisewithin.wordpress.com
© 2008 by Suzan Tusson-McNeil

THIRTEEN VIRTUES

*M*y professional women's group meets once a month for our power breakfast. Today, we read Benjamin Franklin's Thirteen Virtues to set the mood and inspire the creative muse. Joann explained, "I have them taped to my bathroom mirror and think of one each day. Even though Ben admitted that he was never able to live up to the virtues perfectly, he felt he had become a better and happier person having attempted."

Benjamin Franklin's Thirteen Virtues (the short version):

1. **Temperance.** Eat not to dullness; drink not to elevation.
2. **Silence.** Speak not but what may benefit others or yourself; avoid trifling conversation.
3. **Order.** Let all your things have their places; let each part of your business have its time.
4. **Resolution.** Resolve to perform what you ought; perform without fail what you resolve.
5. **Frugality.** Make no expense but to do good to others or yourself; i.e., waste nothing.
6. **Industry.** Lose no time; be always employed in something useful; cut off all unnecessary actions.
7. **Sincerity.** Use no hurtful deceit; think innocently and justly, and, if you speak, speak accordingly.
8. **Justice.** Wrong none by doing injuries, or omitting the benefits that are your duty.
9. **Moderation.** Avoid extremes; forbear resenting injuries so much as you think they deserve.
10. **Cleanliness.** Tolerate no uncleanliness in body, clothes, or habitation.

11. **Tranquility.** Be not disturbed at trifles, or at accidents common or unavoidable.
12. **Chastity.** Rarely use venery but for health or offspring, never to dullness, weakness, or the injury of your own or another's peace or reputation.
13. **Humility.** Imitate Jesus and Socrates.

~ IRIS ADAM
Associate Director of Accreditation and Analytical Studies
The Henry Samueli School of Engineering, University of California, www.uci.edu

✦ ✦ ✦

Our mission statement about treating people with respect and dignity is not just words but a creed we live by every day. You can't expect your employees to exceed the expectations of your customers if you don't exceed the employees' expectations of management.
~ HOWARD SCHULTZ
Chairman of Starbucks Coffee, Co-Author of Pour Your Heart into It

Outstanding leaders go out of their way to boost the self-esteem of their personnel. If people believe in themselves, it's amazing what they can accomplish.
~ SAM WALTON
Founder of Wal-Mart and Sam's Club

Managing Change

Are you ready to make a change? What is the one thing that would make the most difference for you if it were taken care of? Is it a problem that needs to be addressed? Is it an opportunity that would catapult your career, business or personal life to a new level? Do you need to deal with a difficult client, employee or supervisor? Would you benefit from starting a fitness program, paying off debt or scheduling regular time off?

To produce a different result, something will need to change. What you have done up until now has gotten you where you are. Doing the same thing going forward is going to keep you there.

Change can be frightening and uncomfortable. That's why people choose to continue repeating past behaviors rather than risking a change that will take them to their most cherished goal or dream.

The decision to leave the corporate world to start my own business a few years ago was a major change for me. I knew that in order to pursue my dream of helping people become more empowered, fulfilled and successful, I had to make a change. It required me stepping out of my comfort zone and taking risks with no guarantee of success. No doubt, it has been one of the most challenging things I've ever done, but making this change has also led to success and opportunities I would have never imagined.

Is there a change you've wanted to make, but haven't been able to get started? Why not begin today? Here are four tips to help you:

Decide that you will make a change. Hope is not a strategy. Rather than sitting around hoping things will change, decide that you will commit to doing something different in order to create different results in your life, your relationships or your career.

Get clear on your desired outcome. It's hard to hit a target you c see. If you don't know where you are going, how will you know whe you get there? Where do you see yourself once the change has become a reality? What is important about the goal?

Create a plan. Develop a plan to use as your roadmap and guide. It is easier to make progress when you have outlined the steps to take. A clear plan will act as a compass to keep you on course amidst the hundreds of distractions you will face along the way.

Get into action. Once you decide to make a change, it's time to take action. Many people get stuck at this crucial step, letting their fear of the unknown stop them from moving forward. By taking action, you create momentum and positive energy to propel you forward.

What will you do differently? Are you ready to make a change?

~ PAT MORGAN
Life Coach, www.SmoothSailingSuccess.com

✦ ✦ ✦

We are always saying to ourselves . . . we have to innovate. We've got to come up with that breakthrough. In fact, the way software works . . . so long as you are using your existing software . . . you don't pay us anything at all. So we're only paid for breakthroughs.

~ BILL GATES
Founder of Microsoft

ADD SPACE, SYSTEMS, AND SUCCESS
TO YOUR BUSINESS

*A*s women in business, we often struggle for complete control. We might feel that if we can manage the entire project, we can manipulate the desired outcome. Often, the opposite is true. We get stuck in the muck of minutia and lose perspective. Sometimes in order to move forward in life, we have to let go. Letting go of control and possessions can propel us forward into a more fulfilling life.

Muck can mean many things including thoughts that no longer serve us. We grew up thinking that if we worked hard, we would gain success. Who says that success only comes through hard work? What if we earned success by giving our talents to the world joyfully and playfully?

Muck can also be too much stuff. Everything that we own requires energy. Think about one item added to your life that is as basic as a new whiteboard. You purchase a whiteboard to use as a visual aid during meetings. Ok, so you have now managed to get this large item back to your office. Where will it live and how will it be used?

Does it have an easel or will it be mounted to the wall. If it will be mounted on the wall, who will make that happen? If it won't be mounted, where will it and the easel be stored between uses? After all, it's not like you have an open conference room where it can live in between meetings. Ok, so it fits behind the door of your office. Let's hope it also stays upright when you close the door for privacy.

Did you remember to buy the proper markers? How about the eraser? If the board itself is going to live behind your door while not in use, where will you keep the markers so you can find them when you need them? If you can't find the eraser, do you have any extra napkins or paper towels to use in their place? It goes on and on. Get the picture? Even something that is as basic as a whiteboard requires a huge amount of energy and far greater implications in your life than you might have considered.

Protect your life and your psyche from too much stuff. It will pay off in spades. With minimal items to keep track of, your mind can move on to more relevant and fulfilling jobs like attracting new clients or planning for your upcoming vacation.

~ KATHI BURNS
Author, Certified Professional Organizer and Image Consultant
www.AddSpaceToYourLife.com
Excerpt from How to Master Your Muck

✦ ✦ ✦

What does it feel like when someone acknowledges you did a good job? It's worth more than the paycheck! What does it feel like when you know you have gone that extra mile and the client recognizes it and acknowledges it? It makes you want to do it again, doesn't it? As a boss, supervisor or manager stop and think, did you accomplish this tremendous feat all by yourself? You need to take your time and pass on those compliments. Share the love! In addition, look daily at the efforts of staff and find a kind word *to leave behind.*

~ CAROL GRABOWSKI, M.D.

Innovation distinguishes between a leader and a follower.

~ STEVE JOBS
Co-Founder of Apple

How to Take a Good
Picture of Someone

*W*hen it comes to down to it, all any of us want in our lives, is just one, great, image to be remembered by . . . is it too much to ask? And our biggest fear is that we will be caught looking hideous and that is how we will be thought of . . . *forever*!

When we first start out in business, we are always trying to find that one thing we are good at, I was fortunate to find my "good at" thing when I was 20 and became a portrait photographer. When I first started, I asked myself, "What makes an image look great?"

At first I thought, good lighting (bought that), then a cool studio (got that), great equipment (check), then I became skilled at hair and make up and wardrobe . . . still, with all that, I noticed there were photos that had of none of these advantages but still looked great. So I asked myself again, "What is it that makes an image look great?" And the answer came "Capturing the *real* person." *Real*—that's what we love, no fake smiles, *real* ones, no trying to look confident, *real* confidence. How do you get that out of a person? How do you capture that which is secret and guarded?

I'd spend an hour getting everything set up right, putting them together so they look perfect and then stick them out there and say. "Be Real!" My clients just stood there asking me what to do. And at first I really didn't know, I just knew I wanted them to be comfortable and have a fun and successful experience at my studio. I would start telling them a funny story, maybe one that wasn't funny when it happened to me . . . but one that was real. I put on their favorite music. I ask them about their lives, what they like, what they love, whom they love. I devoted myself to them and who they really are, relinquishing and resonating with their individuality . . . creating special moments in my studio where people are truly and deeply connected, connected enough to show me their real self.

So how can YOU *take* a good picture of someone? By first *giving* to them from your heart, then all you need to do is push the button!

~ CECE CANTON
Digital Photographer, www.CeCePhoto.com

We see our customers as invited guests to a party, and we are the hosts. It's our job every day to make every important aspect of the customer experience a little bit better.

~ JEFF BEZOS
Founder of Amazon.com

A business has to be involving, it has to be fun, and it has to exercise your creative instincts.

~ SIR RICHARD BRANSON
British Entrepreneur, Founder of Virgin Enterprises

As we go forward, I hope we're going to continue to use technology to make really big differences in how people live and work.

~ SERGEY BRIN
Co-Founder of Google, and billionaire Internet entrepreneur

Stay committed to your decisions, but stay flexible in your approach.

~ ANTHONY ROBBINS

Lead, Don't Boss Around

*A*s I became a supervisor thirteen years ago and then on moved to higher positions, I learned a numerous leadership qualities not to mention the difference between a manager and a leader. When focused on these areas, all women undoubtedly can become outstanding leaders in their careers. You may have men working with you as peers, reporting to you as subordinates and may be your supervisors. When you are objective in your approach, there is nothing that can pull you down.

Leaders do not order people to do things; instead, they persuade them to accept certain responsibilities, with specific deadlines and agreed-upon standards of performance. When a person has been persuaded that she/he has a vested interest in doing a job well, she/he accepts ownership of the job and the result. Once a person accepts ownership and responsibility, the manager can step aside confidently, knowing the job will be done.

Effective leaders work to put people in the best place for them to thrive and succeed. They mix and match team members to build a well-rounded team that is best suited to the current operating conditions of the organization or the team.

The world hates a "know-it-all," and can spot an overly orchestrated pitch miles away. Your job is to be credible and effective. You don't have to have every answer. Just be good. No one expects you to be perfect.

Your teammates must trust you. You need credibility that assures you aren't perceived in a negative way. Be authentic, truthful, and approachable. Develop an emotional connection between you and your teammates. Be a team player and support others in their growth.

Five Ways To Extend Respect and Dignity to Individuals

1. Value your teammates. When you think about your teammates, place the maximum number on their heads. If we think of others as "10's," we'll do everything to add value to them. Our behavior is totally different when we think of someone else as a "2." Seeing others in the very best light makes the entire team better because usually our level of performance equals the level of value placed on us.

2. Know and relate to what your teammates value. Truly value others as people, and get to know and relate to what others value. Know your teammate's dreams, values, skills, attitudes and personal life situations. If you can extend support to a person's questions, you will invariably find the way to a person's heart.

3. Add value to your teammates. Whatever the project, task or situation, find ways to make others around you better because it is a win/win approach. Making others better isn't just better for others; it's better for everyone.

4. Make them more valuable. Give them the opportunity to learn, contribute and take pride in their contribution. Too many people are still trying to give what they learned years ago. With computerization and globalization there are countless changes. Send them to seminars and classes. Recognize and appreciate. You cannot give what you do not have, so self-improvement precedes team improvement. The first step toward improving the team is to improve you. The only way you can keep leading is to keep growing you. Be current in as many areas as possible.

5. Believe in your teammates. See the potential in your teammates, inspire, and believe in them before they believe in themselves, serve them and add value to them before they add value to themselves.

Cooperation is Collaboration

Perception. Learn to see teammates differently. See them as collaborators, not as competitors.

Attitude. Be supportive, not suspicious of teammates, because if you trust them, you'll treat them differently—you'll treat them better.

Focus. You create victories through multiplication. Concentrate on the team. One is too small of a number to produce greatness. Nothing can be accomplished in a great way without help. Be collaborative. Always listen to your own people.

Mentor

If you take someone under your wing, you're in a great position to make a difference in that person's life. You have the opportunity to provide your expertise to someone less experienced in order to help that person in his/her career. During the process:

1. Don't micromanage. Let them think. Explain the cause and effect, choices and consequences.

2. Don't try to prevent all mistakes. It is good to be proactive and prevent big mistakes, but you have to let the teammate experience some mistakes. Mistakes are learning devices. What they learn from making mistakes will stay with them forever.

3. Don't try to create a clone. Do not try to create another you. Be open to the unique perspectives and talents that they bring to the table.

Communication Styles

Understanding the basic types of communication will help you learn how to react effectively when confronted with a difficult person. You always have a choice as to which communication style you use.

1. Assertive Communicators. The most effective and healthiest form of communication is the assertive style. It's how we naturally express ourselves when our self-esteem is intact, giving us the confidence to communicate without manipulation. These types of communicators work hard to create mutually satisfying solutions. We communicate our needs clearly and forthrightly. They care about the relationship and strive for a win/win situation. They know their limits and refuse to be pushed beyond them just because someone else wants or needs something from us. *Surprisingly, assertive is the style most people use least.*

2. Aggressive Communicators. Aggressive communication always involves manipulation. Aggressive communicators may attempt to make people do what they want by inducing guilt (hurt) or by using intimidation and control tactics (anger). Although there are a few arenas where aggressive behavior is called for (i.e., sports or war), it will never work in a relationship.

3. Passive Communicators. Passive communication is based on compliance and hopes to avoid confrontation at all costs. In this mode they don't talk much, question even less, and actually do very little. People in this style just don't want to rock the boat. Passives have learned that it is safer not to react and better to disappear than to stand up and be noticed.

4. Passive-Aggressive Communication. A combination of styles, passive-aggressive avoids direct confrontation (passive), but attempts to get even through manipulation (aggressive).

By practicing these four types of communication, any woman can be effective in business and walk towards enormous success.

~ VIJAYA "VJ" JAYARAMAN
President, Praevium Research, Inc.

❖ ❖ ❖

Our success has been based on partnerships from the very beginning.

~ BILL GATES
Founder of Microsoft Corporation

It's through curiosity and looking at opportunities in new ways that we've always mapped our path at Dell. There's always an opportunity to make a difference.

~ MICHAEL DELL
Founder and Chairman of Dell Computers

The way to get started is to quit talking and begin doing.

~ WALT DISNEY

My MBA—Mom's Business Advice

*M*y mom never went to business school. She never went to college. In fact, she never even finished high school as World War II broke out when she was in her teens and life was never the same for her afterwards. However, when I started working—and more so when I established my own training and consulting firm—most of the good "business" practices that helped me succeed came from my mom. Let me share seven of her "best practices" with you:

1. Never put off for tomorrow what you can do today.
2. Have a budget (and stick with it) and never spend money that you don't have.
3. Share your knowledge and experience with those who need them.
4. Say what you mean, and mean what you say.
5. Always be willing to lend a helping hand, and go the extra mile for others.
6. Treat everyone respectfully and nicely.
7. Benchmark with others, and continuously raise the bar.

My mom did not sit down and give me these gems of advice all at one time. She probably didn't even have the words to convey these to me. But she did far better. She lived these "good business practices" all her life, and as her daughter, I imbibed them without even being conscious that I was doing so. I never got to thank her for my very own MBA as she passed on last year while I was 10,000 miles away, so sharing with you what I learned from her is my way of thanking her.

~ CELESTE-MICHELLE ALBA-LIM
WLF Interactive Development Centre, www.wlfcentre.com

PASSION HOBBIES

*P*assion Hobbies are pastimes that we do to nurture our spirit and balance our balance. These are activities that brings us joy, enlighten and center, enrich and empower us. For most of us—it's what we do *after* work that helps us keep our sanity *at* work.

Women in my seminars tell me their favorite passion hobbies include: reading mystery or romance novels; walking, running, or aerobics; making needlepoint and crafts for others; jigsaw and crossword puzzles; playing with their kids; and, of course, shopping makes this list every time! I enjoy gathering my women friends for an evening out dancing! It's great exercise, safe and fun.

All the years growing up, I remember my father would rush home from work and head out to the back yard where he would enjoy his passion hobby—organic gardening. He would take out any of his frustrations, find his inner peace, and then come into the house. I know for him (and for us) it allowed time to re-center and re-group from the day, helping him to lead a more balanced life. Today, years after his retirement, it's *still* his passion hobby. A pastime that has nurtured his spirit over the years, and brings a smile every time he shares fresh fruits and vegetables with neighbors, friends and family.

My mother, Beverly Roush, on the other hand, loves to volunteer time to organizations such as the U.S. Olympic Training Center—and she received Volunteer of the Year for her time and energy leading tour groups and helping Olympians pack gear for the upcoming events.

What passion hobbies do you currently have in your life—or could to incorporate into your life on a regular basis that will bring you pleasure, spiritual rejuvenation and greater life balance?

~ SHERYL ROUSH
Speaker, Author of Heart of a Mother, and Heart of a Woman
www.HeartBookSeries.com

SUIT YOURSELF AND BECOME A STAR

*L*ike most career women, I have long suspected that my copy of the standard rulebook is missing several critical pages. In some cases, I think whole chapters must have been removed before the thing was issued to me. Given how out of the mainstream and off-track I often felt over the course of my 20-year legal and business career, it still occasionally surprises me that I was so successful—and that I had such a good time along the way.

I won the game without actually playing it. What I did was play *my* game, and I was successful because I rarely forgot it was their field. Since I kept my eye on the ball, I learned how and when to use my differences, and they became advantages rather than disadvantages.

Part of having a successful and rewarding career is understanding that you're involved in a game with rules—most of them developed by white men a hundred years ago and maintained largely by that same group even today. The rules aren't obvious and women are rarely hardwired with them in the same way men are. You don't have to play by these rules, but you do have to recognize that they exist and that most of the people around you will be playing by them.

As I paid attention and reflected on what worked and what didn't, I also learned that, seen clearly and with perspective, many work experiences and so-called truths really are upside-down and backwards. There is no requirement that women succeed the same way men do, nor is it necessary for all women to succeed the same way. One size does not, and does not have to, fit all. Here are the high-level, differentiating lessons I learned from my career:

- Success is an outcome, not a goal
- The goal is day-to-day contentment

- Satisfaction is an ongoing thing, a process, a way of feeling—it's not a means to an end, it is the end, and it is what you should prioritize
- Success isn't success if it doesn't make you happy
- This is your career and your life, and the only definition of success that matters is yours
- Get rid of guilt as an obstacle to going after what you want—guilt is an unnecessary and unproductive emotion
- Get your choices very clear in your mind, get comfortable with them, and get on with things
- Stay open to redefinition, build flexibility into your system, and give yourself a break—times will change and so will you
- Success is two-sided, and the prize must be worth the price
- All jobs and pursuits have irritants as well as benefits
- You don't get to define what organizations perceive as valuable, but you do get to define what you love to do—it's their field, but you can absolutely play your game
- Like people, organizations have personalities, core values, and structure—recognize this and choose roles where organizational realities work for you rather than against you
- Get yourself in positions where you believe that what you've set out to do can be done, that you can do it, and that it will add value
- Whenever you have a choice or decision to make, ask yourself which route will let you do more of what you love to do and are good at, and less of what you dislike doing, and then choose that route—even if it's not the traditional or expected move
- Stay nimble and able to move, but leave every place better than you found it

- You'll always have more freedom and make a bigger impact if you seek to build the capabilities of the organization and help other people develop instead of trying to do everything yourself
- There's no time for two personalities—be who you are and look to become invaluable
- Your differences are advantages, not disadvantages—view and treat them accordingly
- Be a high-impact performer and find ways to add unique value
- Act like a player rather than a spectator—put some skin in the game and recognize that you get what you give
- Cooperative and collaborative do not equal soft or emotional—they are much-needed differentiators that create competitive advantage
- Get organized and stay organized
- Being busy is not an excuse for being unresponsive and inconsiderate—responsiveness, courtesy, and generosity will get you much farther
- Organizational skills and time management aren't optional—they're necessities that will make your life easier and better
- Focus on what matters most—clear priorities and A+ organizational skills are the keys to success and balance
- Demonstrate leadership every chance you get
- People who act like leaders feel more empowered, more positive, more effective, and more satisfied
- Some lead by ideas, some by energizing groups, some by being in front of the pack, some by coaching from behind the scenes, but everyone has frequent chances to:
  - *Make things better and more fun*

- • *Commit to the success of others*
- • *Fix processes*
- • *Inspire others to want to come to work*
- • *Contribute to strong teamwork, strong culture, and strong organization*
- • Leadership behaviors add unique value—demonstrate them and you'll be happier and more involved, you'll get more money and recognition, and your colleagues will appreciate you more

In my opinion, passion is the name of the game and the fundamental ingredient of a successful and rewarding career. Your career is about your heart, not just your head. Understand that not only *can* you suit yourself and succeed, it's truly the only way to do so. Articulate what matters to you and go for it. Trust other people and give them the gifts of your confidence and support. Get passionate and believe that what is necessary is possible. If you do, you *will* succeed, you *will* achieve the balance you want, and you *will* have a great time along the way.

~ DEBRA SNIDER
Speaker, Author of the novel A Merger of Equals, *www.DebraSnider.com*

✦ ✦ ✦

I feel that one of the best things a person can do for another is to create a job. So you do OK commercially, and then you try to make a difference of some sort.

~ CRAIG NEWMARK
Founder of Craigslist.com, free classifieds website

THE POWER OF "I WANT TO"

*I*n my last corporate position, I was hired as the organizational training manager for a semiconductor corporation and was responsible for the "people side of business." I developed courses in leadership development, personal effectiveness, and team success. After six months, my boss told me the company had decided that I should also manage all aspects of factory training.

I balked.

I had no clue about what went on in the factory. I had no previous experience in this industry and I had successfully evaded anything in my education that could be termed technical. I also knew that the trainers who had previously been managed by manufacturing, had been bumped to process engineering, and finally to human resources before ending up in my lap. This had to be a drain on their morale.

My boss answered my concerns by saying, "Don't worry. It's a no-brainer. It's just three women who come to work, do their jobs, and then go home."

The hair on my back bristled. When was managing anyone a "no-brainer?" I reluctantly accepted the responsibility, hoping to at least provide the three trainers with a more permanent home.

Planning to employ the techniques I taught in my classes, I scheduled an appointment with each one. The first trainer, Cathy, came into my office. As she sat, I asked, "So tell me, what's your vision?"

She looked confused.

I explained, "You know, what do you want for yourself in your job? Is there anything you'd like to learn? Is there something you'd like to do more of or less of on the job?"

She thought about my questions, then said, "There's a new computer system on the floor. I'd love to create some new reporting forms. What we have is so outdated. It would help us a lot if we had a better way to track people and what they're doing."

"Great," I said. "What's it going to take? How can I help?"

"There's a class I can take if you approve the overtime."

We called for the class schedule. After exploring options, we found a way to balance her work with classroom time.

Dina, the second trainer came into my office. Again I asked, "So tell me, what's your vision?"

She looked confused.

I explained, "What do you want for yourself? How would you like to develop and grow? Is there something you'd like to do more of or less of on the job?"

She thought about the question, shifted her body a few times, and then sheepishly said, "I'd like to be a supervisor."

"Great," I said. "What's it going to take? How can I help?"

"I'm not sure."

"Can you ask some of the supervisors on the floor what they think?"

"Sure."

"Good. Find out, come back to me with what you discover and we can work out a plan together." She came back a week later with a detailed plan of training and a commitment by one of the factory supervisors to mentor her development.

The third trainer, Sandy, came into my office. I skipped the vision question. "How would you like to develop yourself and how can I help?"

She shut her eyes and took a breath. Tears began to roll down her cheeks. Finally, she said, "I've worked here sixteen years. This is the first time anyone asked me that."

After these meetings, do you think these trainers acted as my boss had described them, as people who came to work, did their jobs, then left?

Hardly. My greatest problem was managing their overtime. Cathy was rewarded for her new reporting system, Dina became the company's first factory training supervisor, and Sandy committed herself a personal development program that she claimed brought her back from the "living dead." The high evaluations they received from those they trained reflected their renewed motivation to work.

The point of the story is not to tout my success. Success should be given to the management programs I had been teaching over the years; I was just practicing what I taught. The point is that the difference in these employees' productivity had nothing to do with their knowledge and skills. The bottom line was impacted by their emotional commitment. Their performance was based on *how they felt* while doing the job, not on how well they knew how to do it.

It's a simple formula. If *I WANT TO* do a good job, I do it.

If I don't feel like doing a good job, I don't, at least I do not perform up to my maximum potential.

I might do what is required, but my *discretionary effort*—the extra effort that drives a company's competitive edge—rests on *HOW I FEEL* in any given moment.

Do you want only their hands doing the work, or do you want them to put their heart into their work as well? At the end of the day, they are more inspired by how much you care than how much you know.

~ DR. MARCIA REYNOLDS, PsyD
Author of Outsmart Your Brain, *www.OutsmartYourBrain.com*

Tidbits for Top Performance

*T*ake good care of your total health. A person who is not well cannot do well. It is core to your performance. This will sound like your mama preaching to you, but if you want real success, you need to be up for it physically too. It will affect your mental and emotional performance as well. So here are a few tidbits for all of the parts of you:

- Eat on schedule. Don't skip meals, and eat snacks to keep your blood sugar up.
- Choose the right items to eat.
- Stack enough ZZZZZs (a.k.a. get enough sleep).
- Yep, get some exercise regularly. Lots of benefits here for vanity and health and fitness. Also, did you know you lose muscles you don't use and don't "feed" properly? So do both resistance and cardio. They need not be extreme!
- Have occasional yummy treats but make them the exception and not the rule.
- Don't sit all day. Make a point to move around from time to time, even on your break.
- Choose a happy environment. Toxic people will lead to unhappiness. Ask, is it really worth the money to be unhappy? Note: Before you bail out of a work situation, make sure the problem is not yourself. If you find you are often unhappy wherever you work, take a really hard look at yourself and at what makes you tick.
- Do you lighten up the room when you enter it or when you leave it?
- Be accountable. If you say you'll do it, do it.

- Be proactive. If you see a need, offer to help or do it.
- Do your work for your own personal satisfaction. Have pride in your work.
- Find meaningful work—much of your waking life is spent in the work world. Make it count!
- Respect yourself and others. Even if you don't love their personalities. They probably feel the same about you. Why not make it a more positive situation? You do have a choice.

~ ANDREA H. GOLD
www.goldstars.com
© 2008 Andrea H. Gold

✦ ✦ ✦

Your most unhappy customers are your greatest source of learning.
~ BILL GATES
Founder of Microsoft

Whole Foods is dedicated to helping people be healthier and live lives with more vitality and greater sense of well-being.
~ JOHN MACKEY
Founder of Whole Foods Market

Wherever smart people work, doors are unlocked.
~ STEVE WOZNIAK
Co-founder of Apple Computer with Steve Jobs, author of his autobiography called iWoz

Businesswomen & Motherhood

KEEP A POSITIVE ATTITUDE WITH
POSITIVE COMMUNICATION

After a long day at the office, with more work facing you at home, the last thing you might feel like doing is being positive. But it is crucial that, even during conversations aimed at correcting behavior, you keep your tone positive.

What is positive communication? Positive communication is a tool to reinforce good behavior and eliminate bad behavior; it builds self-esteem and inspires confidence in children as well as adults. You can do this, it's easy—once you get the hang of it! Children's feelings of esteem are highly influenced by their interaction and relationship with their parents. You may feel that they are greatly influenced by their peers but the influence of their parents far outweigh that. Everyone has the need to feel loved and accepted, and you can communicate those feelings to your children by the way you speak.

Once you develop the habit of consistent positive reinforcement at home, you'll see that communicating is easier, and you will also be helping your son or daughter learn to communicate with the outside world. By the time they are in elementary school, kids need the self-esteem boost gained when positive reinforcement is in practice.

Suggestions For Communicating with Your Children
- Face your child and maintain eye contact.
- Allow your child to finish talking and complete his statements.
- "Labeling is disabling"—label the behavior instead of the child.
  Incorrect: "Sally, you are a bad girl."
  Correct: "Sally, it is irresponsible to leave your dirty clothes all over the place."

- Help your child learn to talk positively. Start your statements with a reinforcer, such as, "Sara, you are a very bright girl; now, let's talk about the best way to get your homework finished."

Make sure your compliments are truthful. Children, as well as adults, see through false flattery. You will find that these suggestions apply to adults as well as children.

~ DR. ZONNYA
The First Lady of Motivation, Speaker, Author, www.drzonnya.org

✦ ✦ ✦

Increasingly motherhood is being recognized as an excellent school for managers, demanding the same skills: organizing, planning, balancing of conflicting claims, teaching, guiding, leading, motivating, handling disturbances and imparting information.

~ SALLY HELGESEN
Leadership Development Consultant
Author of The Female Advantage: Women's Ways of Leadership

A note to my daughters
If you want advice, you must ask, and you must pay.
And since you asked, balance meditation and activity.
One more word of advice . . . sunscreen.
And finally, when you receive your first paycheck, visit a financial planner, start a book club, and send a love note to a girl friend.
Now you owe me lunch.

~ IRIS ADAM

GIFTS FROM THE HEART:
THE MAKING OF A BUSINESS WOMAN

*M*y mother was a passionate full-time volunteer and my father was an equally passionate entrepreneur. When I was in college, I naturally used the best traits of both my parents when planning my entry into the workforce and starting my career.

I was a studying with a double major in business and sociology. My driving need to make a difference in the world was matched by my eager desire to start earning money. It was my third year at the University of British Columbia when I researched the advertising agencies in Vancouver. I set my sights on a small-sized company that had a broad range of services and clients and was determined to get their attention. After making an appointment with the president of the company, I planned to make an offer I felt he couldn't refuse. Wearing my best professional looking clothes, and with a dangerous level of naïve confidence, I proposed that I would work for their company free of charge for two weeks (and then they would see that they couldn't live without me) and they would hire me full time!

Who knows if it was the bold introduction, the tireless work for two weeks or the unique and clever ideas I contributed that landed me a full time job at the company of my choice. Within a year I opened a Seattle division for the agency and within three years I opened my own marketing communications company, which attracted some of the most desirable accounts in the region. As my firm grew and succeeded, I continued to give back to the community and was honored with numerous awards including an Ethics in Action Award and another for Excellence in Customer Service. After retiring from the industry in which I had built a strong career, I chose to follow my passion and focus my marketing communications skills on professional speaking as well as a health and wellness coaching business.

When I was asked to lecture at business schools and mentor young entrepreneurs, I always encouraged them to give freely of their time before expecting income for their brilliance and I continue to have gratitude for the example my parents gave me. My mother exemplified compassion through her volunteering and my father showed consistent focus that was driving the entrepreneur in him.— a winning combination that is demonstrated in the heart of this businesswoman.

~ JAN MILLS
Health and Wellness Coach, www.JanMills.net

✦ ✦ ✦

Any mother could perform the jobs of several air traffic controllers with ease.

~ LISA ALTHER

Think of stretch marks as pregnancy service stripes.

~ JOYCE ARMOR

People are definitely a company's greatest asset. It doesn't make any difference whether the product is cars or cosmetics. A company is only as good as the people it keeps.

~ MARY KAY ASH
Founder of Mary Kay Cosmetics

GIVING BACK

*F*our years ago a fun and adventurous friend invited my child and me on a mom and child trip to Bali, Indonesia. We had a ball—the shopping, the massages, and the people. The people are so spiritual, kind, and content. Yet they have nothing. We could learn a lot from them. So I stuffed my suitcases and brought home many treasures. Nine trips later I have quite a little import business going!

Now what? Time to give back. An orphanage/school in Bali needs us at Queen Eileen's. Kids in Bali can't go to school unless their parents can pay. There is no public school system. Lots of kids fall through the cracks and when they do, they can spend their whole lives working menial jobs for less than two dollars a day. It is a shame and has become a cycle for generations.

Last year we chose to sponsor two boys from the orphanage so they could go to school. Their mother had passed away from complications in the birth of her second boy. Their father works the rice fields in the early morning hours, then drives a bus until eight in the evening, seven days a week. All this barely covers living expenses for him and his two boys, let alone school. We plan to hold sponsorship of two girls too. For the price of a lunch with my girlfriend we can make a difference in the lives of these kids from the beautiful island of Bali. We continue to take a percentage of our import sales and put it back into the orphanage/school. Not to mention dragging suitcases stuffed with clothing, bedding, toys, books and school supplies each time we visit.

Time to give back? Get involved—just a bag of used clothes and some school supplies can really make a difference. If not this cause—find another one, and support it passionately.

~ EILEEN BURKE
"Queen Eileen," www.QueenEileens.com

WHY WON'T ANYONE HIRE ME?

Having been the typical stay at home '50s mother didn't help when the time came that I decided I needed to go out and find work, work that paid instead of the volunteer hours that gave one a good feeling, but no salary. During that time for the most part, women worked or stayed home and raised a family. My revelation that I was one of few volunteers left in our area occurred when I was constantly being called to help out with this school function or that Little League position, because the other women I had often worked with had now gone into paying jobs and were no longer available.

I was determined to move forward; however, searching out want-ads, applying for jobs, and going on interviews turned into discouraging replies, sorry you don't fit our needs, the job has been filled by someone else, you lack recent experience. This all started in 1975 and at that time employers were free to ask questions about your marital status, your children, their ages, and just about anything they wanted to know. When they found out that my husband was in the Air Force I was told on follow-up calls that we would likely be transferred and they didn't want to spend time and money to train me and then have us leave the area. It's ironic that I live in the same house and location after thirty-eight years. We never moved anywhere.

Times have changed and they can no longer directly ask the type of questions they could then, but employers still have a way of asking to get one to volunteer information to reach conclusions about applicants.

The door to success opened when a friend said she had applied at the county and was taking a test for a clerical position. We both tested and received interviews. I started as a temporary employee with the Assessor's Office and six months later was hired full time. Eight years ago I retired after twenty-seven years of service, no longer in clerical work, but as a senior appraiser.

What I learned was private offices where I had first looked for work couldn't absorb the turnover rate that larger organizations take for granted. Today I have a retirement check as a paycheck and I am free to do what I love, volunteer.

~ RUTH KOEPP

♦ ♦ ♦

Women do not have to sacrifice personhood if they are mothers. They do not have to sacrifice motherhood in order to be persons. Liberation was meant to expand women's opportunities, not to limit them. The self-esteem that has been found in new pursuits can also be found in mothering.

~ ELAINE HEFFNER

The mission statement of my company is to find solutions for families, especially busy moms. I'm reaching out to busy moms because that's what I am. That's what I know, and I know this woman has been underserved.

~ KATHY IRELAND
Model, Kathy Ireland Worldwide

*The company was founded on creating earnings opportunities
for women, even before it went into skincare. The founding Avon
principle, before women could vote and when only men were working,
was to allow women to get out and to create an entrepreneurship
opportunity for them. That was ahead of its time in the 1880s and,
not surprisingly, it was met with resistance. If you fast-forward to
today and the fact that we're the largest source of employment for
women (broadly speaking, as the reps are independent contractors),
we've been an important creator of entrepreneurship for women.*

~ ANDREA JUNG
For Avon, the 21st Century Is Calling

*At work, you think of the children you have left at home.
At home, you think of the work you've left unfinished.
Such a struggle is unleashed within yourself. Your heart is rent.*

~ GOLDA MEIR

*Family is just accident. . . . They don't mean to get on your nerves.
They don't even mean to be your family, they just are.*

~ MARSHA NORMAN

*Women's rights in essence is really a movement for freedom, a movement
for equality, for the dignity of all women, for those who work outside the
home and those who dedicate themselves with more altruism than any
profession I know to being wives and mothers, cooks and chauffeurs,
and child psychologists and loving human beings.*

~ JILL RUCKELSHAUS

The phrase "working mother" is redundant.
~ JANE SELLMAN

Parents learn a lot from their children about coping with life.
~ MURIEL SPARK

Though motherhood is the most important of all the professions—requiring more knowledge than any other department in human affairs—there was no attention given to preparation for this office.
~ ELIZABETH CADY STANTON

I have yet to hear a man ask for advice on how to combine marriage and a career.
~ GLORIA STEINEM

When I got married and had a child and went to work, my day was all day, all night. You lose your sense of balance. That was in the late '60s, '70s, women went to work, they went crazy. They thought the workplace was much more exciting than the home. They thought the family could wait. And you know what? The family can't wait. And women have now found that out. It all has to do with women, or the homemaker leaving the home and realizing that where they've gone is not as fabulous, or as rewarding, or as self-fulfilling as the balance between the workplace and the home place.
~ MARTHA STEWART
Academy of Achievement

I guess I am a little sensitive to the Army slogan "The toughest job, you will ever love!" They obviously know nothing about being a parent.
~ JUDY TEJWANI

You don't choose your family. They are God's gift to you, as you are to them.
~ ARCHBISHOP DESMOND TUTU

Being a full-time mother is one of the highest salaried jobs . . . since the payment is pure love.
~ MILDRED B. VERMONT

Of all the rights of women, the greatest is to be a mother.
~ LIN YUTANG

CHEERS FOR THE VOLUNTEERS

When retired women get together,
They joke and laugh about their pasts,
And they often try to cover up
The fact they'd like their old lives back

They felt wanted then and needed,
They all had talents that they used,
And at home and in the work place,
They worked hard and paid their dues.

This is their time now to relax
(A right they've surely earned,)
Yet they find they can't sit back,
And just watch the world turn.

They need new and different outlets,
For their pent-up energies and skills,
New objectives and new challenges,
A time to give and show good will.

Hospitals, hospices, nurseries,
Libraries, schools, and playgrounds,
Probably would not function at all
If retirees weren't around.

A shoulder, an arm, a helping hand,
A smile, a pat, a caress,
An ear to hear, sweet comfort to cheer,
And tears for another's distress.

And the more that each woman gives,
The more she receives, if you please,
A warm handshake, a hug, a broad grin,
A shy kiss or a heartfelt squeeze.

So retired women must not mourn
That their useful days are done,
Their greatest worth now realized,
And their greatest blessings won.

Hurrahs and cheers for the volunteers,
Who work often times round the clock,
Who shed their own blood, sweat, and tears,
And whose work is worth every drop.

~ VIRGINIA "GINNY" ELLIS
© 2008 Virginia Ellis
www.PoetryByGinny.com

From a Day Job to My Own Job

Changing Limiting Beliefs

As a woman in business I can honestly say I have failed on my way to success and continue learning along the way!

I have been in business for myself for the past fourteen years. The hardest part for me to start my own business was leaving my paycheck, and it was around the same time that my marriage of fourteen years was ending. We had a beautiful home and what looked like success from the outside, but I was very unfulfilled on the inside. I worked in sales and had a cushy paycheck, car allowance, and expense account. I figured once I had enough saved, I could leave my job and start my own business.

I went through that money very quickly not knowing very much about running my own company and as I was now a single mom with two small daughters, I was very overwhelmed!

I made mistakes along the way that cost me not only financially, but emotionally as well. There were nights I cried myself to sleep wondering if I was crazy to pursue my dreams. I thought about giving up because I didn't know if I could do it. Other people would tell me to go get a job and that I wasn't thinking straight. I felt many times that I was letting my kids down when things didn't work, and it was embarrassing and hard to keep going through the rough times. There were literally times I just didn't think I could go on another day.

But I kept connected to the universe or God, however you experience source, and I trusted the gifts inside me were unfolding and somehow things would support me in my life. I felt a deep knowing that I had information inside of me that the world needed and gifts that needed to get expressed to help others.

I believe we all have gifts that need to be shared and so many people go their entire lives too afraid to feel them or don't know how to express them. It may be hard and take courage to do it when you have no idea of *how* and no one is there to encourage you, but I believe that it's harder not to and to ignore yourself. Many people are miserable and their health is suffering or they are in bad relationships because of this very reason, they are not allowing their gifts to unfold and they stay stuck and they don't listen to that knowingness inside, and they "try" to make things work, when deep inside they already know the answers.

Going through those hard times and learning to listen to myself gave me the gift of believing in myself! I learned to trust myself and keep going no matter what the circumstances were. That can be a challenging thing to do, but when I focused on the circumstances I would go into overdrive and, when I stayed connected to the source and *trusted* my maker and listened to the guidance I was constantly being given, it kept me going and kept me strong in myself.

Today I have been blessed with many wonderful friends and supporters in my business and in my life. I still experience challenge, it's part of life, however now I can deal with it differently and more efficiently.

Understanding how you operate and the power of who you are is critical to your business, your success, and your life.

We have many beliefs deep inside that keep us repeating the same thoughts, feelings, and behaviors over and over again. Discovering some of your "limiting beliefs" could produce profound change for your life. Ask yourself these questions in regard to your relationship to money:

- *What do you believe about money?*
- *What do you often say about it?*

- *How do you feel when you spend it or receive it?*
- *Do you think there is enough or do you worry about it?*
- *What messages did you hear growing up?*

Take some time and really explore this for yourself. This is just one topic that continually runs our behaviors on autopilot. We hold on to these old messages as if they are the truth and, until we change those core-limiting beliefs to ones that empower us, we will continue to have the same things and same events occur in our lives.

Most people want to know, how do we change them? That is the key! It's not just about your thoughts; it's about where your thoughts come from! They come from your core beliefs that are stored in your subconscious mind. It's about accessing your subconscious mind and releasing those old messages and empowering yourself "as the adult you today" and filling yourself with new input and new beliefs that will get you the experiences, feelings, and events you really want!

Sit in a quiet place and ask yourself: What is it you need to release in order to _____? And listen to the answers. Don't question the answers or doubt your insight. Continue asking yourself what else you need to know in order to: (produce your results).

I truly believe when you build better rapport with your subconscious mind, you become a stronger, more confident woman! We spend so much time trying to build our business, build our relationships, so begin now to build your inner world and you will manifest everything and beyond! Here's to all the success, love, and bliss that you desire!

~ CAPPI PIDWELL
Master NLP Practitioner and Coach, www.TheAnswerWithin.net

FAME, FORTUNE OR FULFILLMENT—
WHAT FUELS YOU?

*A*s a fired-up young Canadian businesswoman, I wanted it all—"The American Dream"—with a Canadian flair!

In my early twenties, I resigned from the Vancouver-based advertising agency where I began my career. I was driving the brand new luxury sedan, living in the condo with the ocean view and I opened my own event-marketing firm where I worked with some of the most prestigious companies in Canada. I figured I had it all—it was the mid 80s and my clients included international airlines, five-star hotels, and a local circus company that dreamed of performing in other countries (perhaps you've heard of *Cirque du Soleil*?). I was living like a jet-setter, producing events and television shows all throughout North America.

The events were exciting, extremely stressful, and highly lucrative and yet, like a sugar-fix or a few glasses of champagne, the roller coaster of adrenalin became empty and dangerously addictive. The fire required more and more fuel to keep it burning and soon life was like a moving inferno.

Even with this hectic schedule, I was given an opportunity to start making a more meaningful difference with the events I produced.

Immediately following the death of Princess Diana, I was asked to help create a tribute to the most beloved member of the monarchy and the charities she had supported. The whole world was touched by her grace and beauty and we all mourned her tragic death. It was an honour for me to help in a small way to continue her legacy.

The impact of that event was even more life and career changing than I could have scripted or planned. We had symphony orchestras, choirs, and an elegant theatre all donated as a fundraiser for one of the charities she supported. On my way driving to the gala, the unthinkable happened. A drunk driver hit me, head-on! Imagine the irony—enroute to a tribute for a woman killed in a car accident and then I become the victim of a tragic crash.

My injuries from the accident demanded that I change my focus from jet-setting or seeking fame and fortune to more important things like my health and getting out of a wheelchair. The pace was going to be *much* slower and now 100 percent of my focus had to be directed to my physical recovery. Research into health and wellness became a new all-consuming obsession. I learned how to take my recovery into my own hands and when I focused on complementary and nutritional medicine, it became my greatest passion.

After recovering my mobility and regaining my health, I developed a new-found appreciation of wellness and committed to maintaining these priorities in my personal and business life. I became interested in teaching and started to conduct a few workshops to educate others on how to achieve excellence in the event marketing field and then closed that business chapter. Later, I refocused my career on health and wellness coaching, as well as being the keynote speaker at various events. The clients I coach now are no longer faceless corporations. They are individuals who are seeking health and freedom in their personal lives and I'm passionate about helping them achieve those dreams. This successful new career provides fresh inspiration with a sense of meaningful contribution. Today my work gives me a feeling of fulfillment that I never dreamed would be possible.

The following quote from Dr. Denis Waitley summarizes my new philosophy: "Chase your passion, not your pension."

So . . . Fame, Fortune or Fulfillment . . . what fuels you?

~ JAN MILLS
Health & Wellness Coach, www.JanMills.net

Home and the Home Office

Over eleven years ago I became self-employed. At that time my son was going through the limbo period, as I call it. He was too old for day care and too young to drive. As a single mother with an only child, living with guilt became the norm. There were feelings of guilt because I was not there when he came home from school, because he ate too many microwave dinners alone, and guilt because I missed too many band concerts.

It was a major financial gamble when I decided to study weekends for my insurance license and finally started selling long-term care insurance from my home. Though it was not easy at first to meet the mortgage payment, I did gain more control of my time. Maybe I was not always there for my son, but it seemed to be enough for a growing adolescent.

Over the years I have stayed self-employed for many more reasons. It has become my way of life. Along the way I have learned some lessons the hard way.

There are three "musts" that I have found helpful while working in my home. One, you "must" have an excellent certified public accountant to help manage your finances. Two, you "must" keep the office and home as separate as possible; using different phone lines and even computers. Being able to close the door on my office and mentally be focused on home life is essential. And the most important, and sometimes most difficult "must" to remember, is to find time for yourself. By doing something you enjoy, even a bubble bath, you will have more energy for the next "must" do school fundraiser.

~ LYN R. WHITE
Insurance Agent, www.lwhiteinsurance.com

HOW DID I GET TO BE A
LIFE AND BUSINESS COACH?

*I*n 2000, I was sitting next to a bright young man on a flight from Bozeman, Montana to Ontario, California. He had expressed some dissatisfaction with his current sales position. As we talked, I asked him leading questions, hoping to help him see new possibilities. Finally, he said, "Are you a personal coach, by any chance?" I didn't even know what that was.

He produced a business card from his wallet and handed it to me. He said, "I sat next to this woman last week and she was a personal coach. She made me think of new ideas, just like you have."

I returned home, called the number on the card, and hired my own personal coach. I knew right then, I wanted to enroll in coach training and start my own practice. Coaching is a way to help others live life to the max, and the best part is the exceptional people I get to work with. Like the young man on the plane, they are looking to improve their lives or move in a different direction.

My clients pay a monthly fee and call me three times a month for forty-five minutes. Some of them I've never seen face to face. In addition to the calls, we communicate often by e-mail.

I coach clients across the country who are interested in making great strides in their lives. They have the potential to succeed without me, but they enjoy the encouragement and direction as they achieve success at laser speed. I become their personal motivator, sounding board, guide, and cheerleader.

I've coached around career change, weight loss, publishing books and articles, doctoral dissertations, life style change, self-care, fitness, self-confidence, education, public speaking, debt reduction, financial independence, relationships, parenting, profitability, business organization, time management, and more. I've coached speakers, writers, teachers, doctors, financial advisers, mortgage lenders, medical assistants, entrepreneurs, small business owners, artisans, carpenters, college students, school administrators, other coaches, computer technicians, cowboys, bodybuilders, sales reps, paralegals, office managers, missionaries, pastors, and retirees. Their goals are as varied as their areas of interest and employment. From personal foundation to profitability, we plot a course and make giant steps toward the client's desired success.

My clients find it easy to succeed with a coach who holds them accountable, challenges them to think bigger, helps them strategize, and is rooting for them "all the way to the finish line."

I often find myself with a client who wants to start a business from the ground up. So we work on:

- *Business plan*
- *Domain name and e-mail address*
- *Business phone line and/or 800 number*
- *Business address and/or P.O. Box*

- *Business name*
- *Logo*
- *Business cards*
- *Web site*

This process can be daunting, but with a coach's encouragement, it can move along rapidly. Taking Giant Steps Brings About Success in a Hurry.

~ KAREN ROBERTSON
Speaker, Author, Coach, www.giantstepsuccess.com

MY MID-LIFE CAREER CHANGE

Opportunity

On March 30, 1981, the day John Hinckley attempted to change the U.S. government by shooting President Ronald Reagan, my husband learned that he had landed a job with an international oil company in The Netherlands (Holland). It was an opportunity of a lifetime for our family. The company would pay our moving expenses and the tuition to a prestigious private school for our children.

I looked forward to the opportunity to travel but had to struggle with my dreams. I was one semester short of graduating from college with a degree in health care administration. I wouldn't be able to work due to the Dutch tax and labor laws.

We left our spacious two-story home in Orange County, California, and shoehorned our large American style furniture into a narrow three-story row house in the city of Leiden. The living room had an enormous picture window that looked out on the Rhine River canal only a few feet from our back door. Holland is built below sea level. If the country's dikes broke, the North Sea would flood the lowlands and we'd be in water to our rooftop. I tried not to think about it.

I stepped outside and walked around our building. I jumped in alarm when something struck me. A fish fell on my head and bounced to the ground, flopping its tail. A seagull swooped down, grabbed the fish and flew off with it.

I went inside to unpack my typewriter. I wrote about life at twenty feet below sea level in a country that rained fish. I wrote about the Rhine River in our back yard, about the kids' prestigious private schools housed "temporarily" in a former prison. I wrote about the crazy squatters in the row house at the far end of our building and their lush marijuana plants on the back patio facing the police station on the other side of the canal. I wrote about doctors who make house calls and who recommended a daily dose of fresh air and sunshine in a land of fresh rain and endless clouds.

Changing Seasons

I was getting dressed in our second story bedroom one morning when I realized that someone was watching from what appeared to be beyond our balcony. An enormous barge rose high out of the canal. Three kids were playing inside a fence on top of the barge. They looked down at me through our second story windows as they floated down the river.

A few days later, the same barge returned, heavily laden, riding low in the water. I looked down from our balcony. A lighted window and curtains revealed the kids and their mother in the tiny kitchen. Father was somewhere in the huge barge, steering it up the river.

The barges went back and forth until winter, when the canals froze over. We ice skated on the river. It was fun and cold. We stopped when someone announced "ollibollen" and fished out a hot steaming doughnut ball from a deep pot of boiling oil, rolled it in powdered sugar and handed it to us in a paper wrapper. It warmed the hands. After a few hesitant, but very eager, nibbles, we devoured them.

Eventually we would hear a loud crushing sound growing closer and closer. An enormous icebreaker roared by, clearing a passage for the barges that followed at a respectful distance.

Spring and summer brought sailboats and tour boats.

The canals brought tragedy. Our son's best friend dove into one of the canals without checking the depth first. He struck his head on a sandbar and fractured his neck, rendering him a quadriplegic.

Dutch Lessons

Several rowdy teenagers jumped onto the tram I was riding, shouting insults at one another. One was particularly funny and I laughed. They stared at me, puzzled, because I looked too American to understand their language. Most Dutch people know English and it's possible to spend five years in the country and never learn its language.

Our kids picked up the language on the street and spoke it with the neighbor kids. I took Dutch lessons with other adults. The Germans, Romans, and Spaniards occupied the country at one time or another. I had studied German, Latin, and Spanish, so Dutch was fairly easy to learn.

Our Dutch teacher looked serious when she came in one day. She handed out several pages of Dutch phrases and hand signals. Eyebrows went up and eyes grew large. "This is what your kids are saying," she said, "You need to know what it means." She was right. We had a family meeting that night.

The Biggest Hurdle

Before leaving the U.S., I looked into colleges that had business school programs in The Netherlands. Michigan State had an International Law program that fit my needs perfectly. I didn't have to postpone finishing business school for five years, after all.

This, the greatest hurdle to me in deciding to make the move to Holland, turned out to have the greatest value when I joined the business world a few years later. I had six months of intensive courses in International Law. Our faculty leaders took us on behind-the-scenes tours that few people ever see.

We toured the Peace Palace and the International Court of Law in The Hague. We were briefed on a current trial at the Court of Justice of the European Communities in Luxembourg. We sat in the Debating Chamber at the Council of Europe. We listened to lectures on the current state of the world economy at the International Chamber of Congress in Paris.

In 1986, the year we returned from Holland, I was doing some research on the Dutch health care system at the University of Leiden Medical School Library. I turned a page of the medical journal I was reading and discovered a half-page advertisement for an upcoming conference of the American Medical Writers Association. I didn't know what a medical writer did, but I knew I was one.

When my husband's job ended and we returned to California, I went back to school and got a master's degree in health care administration. When a medical writer position opened up at a local company, I had the skills and education. Over the next twenty years I worked in a pharmaceutical and a medical device company in several departments: clinical research, marketing, and as a manager of a global scientific communications department. I left the corporate world two years ago to become a freelance writer.

I didn't give up a career to go to Holland. I discovered who I was.

~LANIE M. ADAMSON
Freelance Writer, www.LanieAdamson.com

✦ ✦ ✦

We can tell our values by looking at our checkbook stubs.
~ GLORIA STEINEM

WHAT IS YOUR OCCUPASSION?

I was not one of those kids who knew what she wanted to do when she grew up. I actually envied the kids who did. Sure, many kids say they want to be a doctor, ballerina, or firefighter and change their minds when they get older.

But, I remember one of my girlfriends in elementary school who said that she wanted to be a flight attendant when she grew up. That same girlfriend still wanted to be a flight attendant in junior high and high school. Sure enough, when she graduated from high school she went on to work for a major airline. She still loves being a flight attendant. It's what I call her "occupassion."

We're not all like that, though. I certainly wasn't. I didn't realize my calling, so to speak, until I was forty-two years old. I used to secretly think that there was something wrong with me because I'd start looking for something else whenever I was in position for a few years. The realist in me seemed to always pursue jobs within the same field, but that thing in me that wanted to feel fulfilled by the work I did still yearned for something—something it wasn't getting.

Then I had my son. When he was about nine months old I began to question everything I was doing. I started to entertain the idea of working from home. It became a very appealing notion. So, I researched various ways I could generate an income from home. It took years for me to get to the point where I do work from home full time. Sometimes it felt like I was taking two steps forward and then one step back, but, I kept at it and did realize my dream.

During that process, something else happened. I came to realize that I was at a point where I simply was no longer willing to do work I did not enjoy doing. This realization, this shift in what I was committed to in my life—doing work I love—was a mindset that was critical to me finding my occupassion.

Now, I understand that this may sound like a luxury—refusing to do work you do not like doing. It's not, though. It's essential to our overall well-being. Just think about what kind of world in which we would be living if we all loved the work that we did. It really is not a grandiose idea.

Does this mean that I do not do any work related activities that I would rather not do? No, of course not. There are things that I do here and there, through the course of my workday that I'd rather not do. But, overall, the work I do is extremely fulfilling for me. And, it may be the case that the work I'm doing today is leading me to something else I may do in the future. Today I'm okay with that because the path that I've led has been a wonderful journey.

So, I leave you with some questions to ask yourself to help you along with your journey: What are you passionate about? Are you willing to take a few risks to see how you might turn that passion into a way to earn income? Do you like yourself enough to give yourself the opportunity to have your occupassion?

~ KIMBERLY ANNE
© 2008 Kimberly Anne

✦ ✦ ✦

Every blade of grass has its angel that bends over it and whispers, grow, grow.
~ *THE TALMUD*

Entrepreneurial Spirit

LET YOUR BUSINESS LEAD YOU

Let your business lead you.
Let it guide you
to those places in your heart you have yet to discover.
Let it call your soul
to be fully expressed and engaged in the world.
Let it be the way
for you to contribute your unique gifts to the world.
Let it be your tool
for making the planet a better place.
Let it be your vehicle
for leaving a legacy long after you are gone.
Let it be *you* . . .
mind and body, heart and soul.

~ CHRISTINE KLOSER
Author, The Freedom Formula: How to Put Soul in Your Business and Money in Your Bank,
Love Your Life LLC, www.LoveYourLife.com

All entrepreneurs begin with three categories of means:
1. Who they are—their traits, tastes, and abilities
2. What they know—their education, training, expertise, and experience
3. Whom they know—their social and professional networks.

Using these means, the entrepreneurs begin to imagine and implement
possible effects that can be created with them.

~ SARAS D. SARASVATHY
University of Washington School of Business, Harvard Business Review
© 2001 Saras D. Sarasvathy

BACK TO WHERE I BEGAN ...
TO FIND THE HEART OF MY BUSINESS

It seems like a lifetime ago ... I graduated college with a degree in elementary education, because my mom thought I'd be a great teacher: "You can always go back to teaching." Yet, working in a classroom with thirty screaming kids was the furthest thought on my mind. Although I enjoyed my years of learning, I never developed a rapport with elementary school kids. They had too many disciplinary problems for me to be able to teach them much of anything. And they hadn't taught us much about managing behavior in the classroom.

So I pursued my second choice, the next best career to teaching—marriage! Since my husband was in the service, we moved a few times, and I settled for part time clerical jobs wherever we lived. When we settled in California after he served his time, we got into retailing where I stayed for ten more years after our divorce. (California may have something in the water that breaks up marriages!)

Although managing clothing stores was fun, I'd always had the heart of an artist, so besides enrolling in all variety of craft classes, I took continuing courses in creative writing. I had written since I could hold a pen—poems, music, and school plays. I even crafted my own little books and read them to my friends. As an adult, I nurtured my natural writing gifts through ongoing writing classes at the local universities. I loved my writing assignments and felt more alive when putting words on paper than at any other time. I was thrilled when some of my creations won prizes in a few of the contests I entered.

By 1984, I quit my last retail job to pursue my writing more seriously. In order to have the time to write and still bring in income, I started several "cottage" industries including organizing, desktop publishing, and bookkeeping, none of which really nurtured my creative spirit. But as long as I could keep writing, I was creatively fulfilled.

In 1988, my writing teacher invited the class to attend a school play which we were to critique for an assignment. I found I loved writing reviews—which meant giving my two cents—and shortly thereafter created my first paid gig writing video reviews for a weekly newspaper. After a fun year of seeing my name in print, I turned my "clips" (copies of my published articles) into a two-year stint as a columnist for a slick local magazine with a definite pay raise! Now I was hooked. I got to go out and play "ace reporter" as I interviewed minor celebrities, politicians, and community members of long standing.

Throughout this time, I had also written several books and was sending them to publishers, subsequently building a huge collection of rejection slips. After too many years of rejections, I finally got smart and hung out my shingle as a ghostwriter. I would write books for others and get paid up front, whether or not their book ever got published or sold a single copy.

Since I had effectively been self-employed since 1984, I was comfortable setting up my ghostwriting business and actually enjoyed writing for others almost as much as I did writing my own material. Although I started off with limited confidence since I had never written books for others, my skills were confirmed when I won the San Diego Book Award for the best "how to" book in 2001. I walked up on stage to accept my reward as if I were receiving an Oscar. It felt that good!

From there it only got better. I continued ghostwriting as well as copyediting books, articles, newsletters, press releases, website content, and eventually e-books and other information products.

The "info-product" boom was exploding, with e-books growing in popularity even as Amazon announced the development of their e-book reader. These "books" were not printed on paper but delivered electronically, that is, someone would buy the e-book and then get to download it immediately. This offered instant gratification to the purchaser and pure profit to the seller—the author/publisher who doesn't have to pay printing costs.

Because I was writing a lot of e-books, a business colleague approached me to co-teach a "webinar" on creating info-products. She knew I had been teaching occasional writing classes through the adult school system. What she did was rent a piece of cyberspace where she has a virtual room that people attend to hear and see a lesson. The webinar is truly a virtual classroom with the ability for the teachers to deliver the lecture, put up slides, and interact with the students.

My partner and I loved giving the webinars and did so for a while until we took a break. Next, almost simultaneously three events occurred: I was hired to write the workbook and course material for a three-day intensive on Internet Marketing for Women; from that I got the inspiration to teach a three-day intensive on creating info-products in my partner's webinar room; and I was hired by UCSD to teach an online marketing course for copyeditors. Everything seemed to be pointing back to teaching. Wow, I never expected that!

Today, I feel like I've come full circle from graduating college as an education major and rejecting teaching children in a classroom to building a writing and editing business where I'm now teaching adults in cyberspace. What's so great about this 360° turn of events, is that I found I really love teaching—when it's a subject I'm passionate about, when I can communicate with students I have rapport with, and when I can do it all from the comfort of my home office. It doesn't get any better than that. Well, I could be a bestselling author. That's coming . . . .

I never imagined I'd go back to where I began . . . to find the heart of my business.

~ ANDREA SUSAN GLASS
www.WritersWay.com

❖ ❖ ❖

The entrepreneur is our visionary, the creator in each of us. We're born with that quality and it defines our lives as we respond to what we see, hear, feel, and experience.

~ MICHAEL GERBER
Entrepreneur, Author of The E-Myth Revisited

I charge a price for my services that is commensurate with my knowledge, experience, and abilities. All of my clients are pleased with my work. My highest purpose is to be true to myself. When I honor my personal gifts and talents, I fulfill my destiny and serve others at the same time.

~ LOUISE L. HAY
Interviewed on Oprah (July 2008)

No one can make you feel inferior without your consent.

~ ELEANOR ROOSEVELT

CLASSROOM OF LIFE

Business schools, workshops, seminars. and boot camps abound today. Everyone is going off to attend something somewhere. Perhaps what we need most is a retreat—one back to our childhood.

Being an eight-time entrepreneur, I can attest to the best business school courses worthy of consideration, with the lowest tuition yet the highest return.

Some of the most valuable ethics were those role modeled by my mother. To support the family income, and to get her out of the house being a young stay-at-home mom, she was the door-to-door Avon lady. Since my two brothers were old enough to attend school, she carted me around on her weekly routes. Believe it or not, I was quite shy, so she made me meet people—which translated later into natural networking skills.

A few years later, to help put my brothers through college, mom starting selling Amway products, and our household was one of the first to use biodegradable products—a truly novel "green" concept at that time. When I was fourteen, she dragged me to an Amway "Revival" where I heard my first motivational speaker, Charlie "Tremendous" Jones. Today, we are colleagues in the National Speakers Association, and I'm a motivational speaker! From painfully shy to inspirationally high! (We never know where the seeds are going to be planted.)

From mom, I learned Midwestern values, work hard, show respect, do right, have integrity, help others, and what I now know as good old-fashioned customer service skills.

"Know what you want in life—and go for it." A child of the Depression, at eighteen, mom moved herself from the farm in Iowa, with only $10, and her best girlfriend to "get a life" in California. She taught me

about goal setting and visualization, without ever using the phrases. (I was named after that best girlfriend.)

"Be positive." Attitude truly does make a difference in our ability to succeed—I'm convinced of that! In challenges where I have not yet developed the skills, it's been having a positive attitude that has catapulted me through the fears. As a speaker on the topic today, I believe that faith is the "compass" of attitude. We've also got to believe in ourselves.

"You can do anything you put your mind to." A secret dream of mom's was to compete in the Olympics. At sixty-eight, she was selected to carry the Olympic Torch, on its way from San Diego to the 1984 Los Angeles Games. When I started a business at age sixteen on the patio of my parents' home, she encouraged and helped me with the silk-screening of t-shirts and bumper stickers. (My first client was the Shriners.)

"Use what you've been given." We each have skills, talents, and unique abilities. As a youth, I was a graphic artist with a typewriter and mimeograph paper. (Remember those?) Mom constantly volunteered me to donate time designing the boating club and church newsletters. Later I earned four international design awards for newsletters, have written five books, and have presented seminars in eight countries on the topic. It's as if she knew . . . .

The best business school courses I've ever attended have been those in the classroom of life with mom as my teacher.

~ SHERYL ROUSH
Speaker, Author, Daughter of Beverly J. Roush
wwwSparklePresentations.com
© 2008 Sheryl L. Roush

CREATIVE SUCCESS

*W*omen have a natural instinct for business, leadership, and entrepreneurship. We are also multitasking experts. As far back as biblical times we find women described as business experts, entrepreneurs, and multitaskers. The "Proverbs 31 Woman" is reflected as a wise woman in business: *"She considers a field and buys it; from her profits she plants a vineyard."* —Proverbs 31:16

As a veteran of the U.S. Air Force, I learned leadership techniques, top-notch networking, and management skills. Women make up about 20 percent of the military today, compared to only 8 percent when I enlisted in October of 1980. I was trained as a contracts specialist in purchasing, negotiation, and administration of contracts. I was a high school dropout who was told by my teachers and parents that I would never amount to anything. Born to two alcoholic parents, I grew up neglected and abused. The military was my saving grace and I fought hard against that "loser" expectation, excelling in my military career. I became a leader, manager, and networking expert. I earned two associates and a bachelor's degree while on active duty as well as the highest level of professional certification in my field.

Using my skills and expertise, I developed some additional streams of income on the side. An enlisted military salary is a modest income and finding ways to earn extra cash gave me more flexibility and afforded me more opportunities in life. I used my creativity to come up with clever ways to earn extra money. In the late 80s I started a home-based cosmetics business to get over my fear of public speaking. I knew I would be giving presentations in college and was often required to give military briefings to higher-ranking officials.

Have you ever been petrified of something? I was absolutely petrified to speak in front of people. I had an extremely negative self-image from my upbringing and was unable to speak to a group without panicking and feeling nauseated. My first presentation was to one of my close friends. The information was all right in front of me on a flip chart, and all I had to do was read. I stuttered through the entire presentation. There is a point where you must decide to give up or persevere. I wanted to give up but I pushed forward and managed to reduce the fear, and earn some extra income.

In May 2002, I deployed to the Middle East for four months after 9/11 and chose to retire in April 2003 after twenty-three years of honorable military service. My retirement speech was given with confidence and ease. I discovered I liked public speaking! The transition out of the military was difficult. The real world seemed foreign to me. I had spent my entire adult life up to this point in the military system, which is an institution. Upon retirement, I immediately went to work for a defense contractor handling government contracts.

I made a good salary along with my military retirement, but still found I enjoyed being entrepreneurial. I started a home-based travel business and have done quite well with that, as I enjoy traveling myself and help others travel at wholesale.

Getting restless in my corporate job, I knew in my heart that sitting behind a desk was not my path to success. I'd had a horrendous childhood and experienced abusive relationships in my teen and adult years. I worked hard to make significant changes and completely reinvent myself and turn my life around. The secret to life isn't what happens to you but what you do with what happens to you. I have an intense passion to help others turn their lives around and am developing my current business model around that.

Knowing that I would be speaking and sharing my story, I joined Toastmasters as a way to improve my skills. I won three contests and made it all the way to the district-level competition. I started working with a nonprofit and speaking on how to raise money and awareness for domestic violence issues.

Each step taken away from a behavior that doesn't serve you is a step toward success. I took the step toward getting over my fear of speaking which was the difference that made a difference. Today I'm an award-winning speaker, on the board of and the voice of the Women's Peace Campaign, a certified master results coach, consultant, and up and coming author.

The secrets to my business and personal success have been to integrate three primary philosophies to achieve maximum results. First, surround yourself with people who hold you to a higher standard. These people will challenge you and encourage you to keep moving forward to your success. Next, eliminate negativity from your life, thoughts, words, actions, and people. Negativity will absolutely stagnate your success and prevent you from moving forward in a positive direction. Finally, release any and all resentment you carry.

The key to success isn't what you know or whom you know but who you are to whom you know. People will remember honesty, integrity, dependability, and an impeccable word above all else. Be true to your word, be honest with those you meet, be dependable, and do all things with excellence and integrity. When you are wrong, promptly admit it and ask for forgiveness. Take responsibility for your actions. Finally, never quit, never give up, and never let go of your dreams. You can be the light of the world to just one person. Let your light shine and be the difference that makes a difference and watch all your dreams come true.

~ ELDONNA LEWIS FERNANDEZ
Speaker, Coach, www.pinkbikerchic.com

Broadcast Your Passion

My mother was ill in the ICU for three weeks and in the hospital for six months. When she was lying there with all the tubes around her, I started to worry that she was not going to make it. I didn't want to admit it, but I started thinking about it in my quiet time. And, I wondered if she didn't make it, had she done the things she wanted to do in her life? Had she reached her goals? Had she reached her dreams? Was she living the life she wanted to live or was she living her life for my Dad or me?

While I was asking her those questions, I was also asking myself, and unfortunately my answer was no. I wasn't living my dream. I hadn't really done anything, except have my children and get married. I hadn't done anything that I felt was important, or exciting and I wasn't leaving any kind of legacy. It was time for me to start giving back. I thought, "How am I going to do it?" I decided to go out and reach women like myself—women fifty-plus—by bringing people to them who had reached their dreams so these women would know they don't have to settle for where they are in life. I wanted to help them see they can create their income, get through being abused, get through their trials and tribulations and turn them into triumphs. I wanted extraordinary women to share not only their success but their how to's. A few weeks later, right there in the hospital waiting room, my radio program was born!

You can create your own radio show to promote your business and reap the benefits and exposure to grow your business by establishing you as an expert, building a platform to market products and services and creating a new revenue stream. How? Start by discovering your true passion or purpose. What makes you happy and excited so you jump out of bed in the morning? What lit you up as a child? What message or cause do you have a burning desire to share? What have you always wanted to do? Be authentic—be true to your purpose. Don't try to be an Oprah, Larry King, or Ellen. Be yourself. Your audience will appreciate it and be attracted to who you are.

Identify your target audience. Deliver one-to-one on radio. Don't talk at your listeners, speak with them. Picture your perfect audience and be in alignment with their needs. Your message should clearly speak to them.

Choose your format. Your show can be one minute or one hour long. Some of the most successful are twenty minutes—the average commute time! If you are interviewing others, the combination of voices is entertaining and people will listen longer. Another option is a panel discussion, like The View. Pick a topic and have two to four people discuss it. If you're an author or speaker you may want to use the commentary format. Take a portion of your book, speech, or tele-seminar and deliver it in small, bite-sized pieces.

Preparing for your show. For interviews, choose a topic and find the perfect guest for your topic. Consider experts in your field of interest that will appeal to your audience. Choose a target date for launch. Send press releases and promote at least two weeks prior to your launch. Now, it's your time to shine! Start broadcasting your message globally and unleash the power of your voice—broadcast your passion!

~ RAVEN BLAIR DAVIS
Executive Producer/Host, WomenPower-Radio, www.WomenPower-Radio.com

Being the Right Person in the Right Place at the Right Time

The turning points in my life were unplanned and out-of-the-blue, but I was ready for them. When I was sixteen, a girlfriend said, "I'm going to be an actress." A thunderbolt flashed over my head and "Me too!" flew out of my mouth. At that moment, I became an actress and although I didn't know how I was going to make it happen, I found my way. Within a few years, I was a New York-based professional stage actress, performing in thirty-three productions throughout the United States, sometimes sharing the stage with big film stars—not because I had an action plan but because of "Me too!" I was being true to my word. There's power in being.

And magic. Before moving to New York, as a university graduate in Chicago, I needed a union card. I had no idea how I was going to get one but I went on auditions for everything—print work, hair modeling, voice-overs, films, plays, commercials, industrials, you name it. Once I was auditioning for a musical and was in the ladies' room warming up my voice. When I walked out, a gentleman was standing there, waiting to meet me. He was the producer, had been walking by, liked what he heard, and ended up casting me. Because of this job, I got my Actors' Equity card, entered the professional ranks and soon got a position with a theater company that moved me to the East Coast. I was the right person in the right place at the right time—just being and doing what I loved.

Eventually I was ready for more, but didn't know what. I relocated again and was working in the theater box office at Los Angeles City College. A professor and I struck up a conversation and I shared about my acting background. He asked to see my resume and immediately asked if I would be interested in teaching voice and speech at the

West Coast American Academy of Dramatic Arts, where he was the department head. I had never thought about being a teacher, but accepted his invitation and still remember my first day on the job. I had landed on the shore of my life's work!

Today, my passion for teaching still burns brightly. It's three decades later (three blinks of an eye) and as an adult education instructor, corporate trainer, and executive coach in communication skills, I have worked with thousands of professionals from every industry, in the U.S. and abroad. This, in turn, has prepared me to write *Speak with Passion, Speak with Power!*, my workbook for transforming inexperience and the fear of public speaking into energy, know-how, and results, which I use in my public speaking courses and trainings.

What I've learned from my life and work is that the key to having both steady growth and quantum breakthroughs is preparation, persistent preparation, and continuous readiness. Being the right person in the right place at the right time is not accidental. It comes out of who you've become, and being powerfully in action, which turns you into a human magnet who attracts the right people and circumstances into your life.

This is the key to powerful communication too. Communicating is taking action and whether you're delivering presentations, leading teleconferences or webinars, interviewing for positions, teaching courses, managing others—whenever you're communicating for results—ask yourself "Who am I being?" "Am I being the message?" "Am I being the purpose?" "Am I being effective?" "Am I being a contribution?" Answering these questions requires you to be accountable to your listeners, to do what works, and drop what doesn't.

It works to be prepared and this is the focus of my courses. Students model what it means to be extraordinary communicators by repeatedly preparing and practicing brief presentations with each other, before going in front of the whole group. They coach each other, asking, "Is your purpose clear?" "Are you being congruent in your delivery?" Partners give and receive feedback based on body language, voice, ideas and organization, energy and inner state, because these work harmoniously together in extraordinary communicators.

Many presentations, practice sessions and partners later, distracting behaviors and limiting patterns, including procrastination and perfectionism, are replaced by greater self-confidence and self-mastery. Students train themselves to do what works, to be prepared, and have better results.

Sometimes before an individual is ready to be an extraordinary communicator, they need to overcome an intense fear of public speaking. At this point, they're afraid of the fear, so I coach them to face it, get familiar with it, build a tolerance to it and work with it. They shift into being neutral about having fear and this allows room for them to be prepared for success and extraordinary.

If a client is interviewing for a position, they must be "The One!" and have the interviewer get it: "I'm the one who's going to solve your problems, make you look good and here's why." I help them identify what isn't the right person, right place, and right time—right down to what they're thinking, visualizing, and feeling. When these are brought into alignment, a powerful force field is created.

When your outside and your inside are one and the same, you're congruent and a powerful human magnet. This is why preparation is the key, persistent preparation, continual readiness. Actions issue from who you're being and both lead to steady growth and to unplanned, out-of-the-blue breakthroughs. So follow your heart, live a life consistent with your vision, and opportunities will appear. They have for me and like Shakespeare said, *"The readiness is all."*

~ PAMELA KELLY
Teacher, Coach, Author, www.pkelly.com

✦ ✦ ✦

ROLLER COASTER

Today, I own and operate the most fun store on earth called Queen Eileen's. Before that, no college—just the school of hard knocks—a lucrative career as a stripper for fifteen years in Miami—bad marriage—dumped Mr. Wrong and met Mr. Right— have the perfect child—opened our shop. I plopped my four-day-old kid down in a bassinet and here we are! A roller coaster—Fun Fun Fun! Crazy long hours and great folks. Both customers and employees become like family. While the rest of the world is at the beach during the summer, I'm finishing up my Christmas orders. Things can be stressful as well. Many times I hold off cashing my paychecks so my team can cash theirs. The next time you are in your favorite store look around and know that most of all you see is not yet paid for and someone is probably losing sleep over it. I'm still loving it!

~ EILEEN BURKE
"Queen Eileen," www.QueenEileens.com

The Entrepreneur

I used to spend a lot of time trying to impress,
Little did I realize how it added to my stress.

My zealousness for business and my desire to succeed,
Led me at times to stretch the truth, exaggerate, mislead.

Name-dropping, bragging or a little white lie,
It's harmless I'd say, I must impress, or at least try.

My home is the biggest, I make lots of money,
My spouse the most wonderful, my world is sunny.

Look at me! Look at me! Do you think I'm great?
I'm not quite sure, how do I rate?

Later I'd lament that all was not well,
What in the world was I trying to sell?

It was then that I learned as I worked with my coach,
That perhaps what I needed was an adjusted approach.

Be humble, speak the truth, understate, promise less,
This new way of thinking would be key to success.

As I shifted my focus and turned inward to grow,
I discovered the truth that I had longed to know.

I'm truly enough, just as I am, being me
No exaggeration necessary, WOW, I feel free!

~ PAT MORGAN, LIFE COACH
www.SmoothSailingSuccess.com

Never Underestimate
the Power of a Purse

I launched *Mars and Venus Starting Over* across the room after reading the part about how forgiving your cheating ex-spouse sets you free. Depressed, miserable, and downright cranky, I was trying to navigate life after an unexpected divorce. How can I move forward?

While I knew that accessorizing was one of my strengths, I didn't know it would be my salvation. Like many women, I have always loved fashion and after reading an article about following your passion, I decided to design fun purses and scarves. Sprawled out on the den floor with a deconstructed purse and the fashion channel blaring, I cut into silks, cottons, and anything else that caught my fancy. The process of transforming flat colorful fabric into functional, unique accessories was the first thing that brought me joy in months. Tapping into a creative part of me that had been dormant during my marriage and realizing a beautiful, tangible result not only helped me weather a tough time, it enabled me to flourish.

As I was ending one chapter of my life, I gave birth to "n. bahr designs," or as I thought of it: "fashion as therapy." Though I continued my full-time work in the non-profit arena, I started to sell my creations to stores. I even received media attention for my company. One such article chronicled my journey: Director of Development for the Delaware Museum of Natural History by day and accessories designer by night.

Three years into this journey, I unexpectedly met a handsome Brit who wanted to order some purses for his nieces. (Okay, maybe he also wanted something else.) A year later, we married and moved to southern California.

Now, eight years after its creation, my company continues to grow, as do I. I have added funky "Dr. Suessian" Christmas stockings and vibrant belts. I have developed a website and marketing materials and joined a wonderful women's business group. My work has been in galleries and stores on both the East and West Coasts.

Oh, and the Brit, he is the love of my life. For our first Christmas, he surprised me by buying my domain name to create a website. He is my biggest advocate and cheerleader. I am grateful every day that an unexpected ending led to a passion that not only guided me through one of the most difficult periods of my life, but also helped me succeed professionally and personally.

Never underestimate the power of a purse.

~ NANCY BAHR KELLY
n. bahr designs, www.nbahrdesigns.com

◆ ◆ ◆

The five essential entrepreneurial skills for success: Concentration, Discrimination, Organization, Innovation and Communication.

~ MICHAEL GERBER
Entrepreneur, Author of The E-Myth Revisited

To find your path, ask the Universe: "How can I be used?" "What do you want from me?" (Not the other way around.)

~ OPRAH WITH MARCUS BUCKINGHAM
On Oprah, referencing Eckhart Tolle's work

The Tree Farm:
An Extended Family

*W*hat do you do with an unusual business, a home, and five children? You just do it. And I did it for ten years, during the 60s and 70s and had the time of my life. At that time I didn't think so. It was hard work. I was a farmer, a mother, and learning so much.

How did I find myself in this situation? I didn't plan it. I had a home, and next to it five acres on which I grew and sold Christmas trees. My children, who ranged in age from three to fourteen, learned to help with the "farm." Often they surprised me with their ingenuity with their chores.

The plan for each year was to plant new trees and prepare the more established trees for sale. Mostly that was my job. I was good at shaping the trees and enjoyed making them look like upside-down ice cream cones. The children couldn't fill all the needs so I turned to local high school and college students. At the peak of my enterprise, I hired seventeen young people. Although each one had a life beyond the work they did on my tree farm, I treated them as an extension of my family. Since my home was next to the farm, it was natural to prepare lunch for them. My ability to put together large quantities of food was an advantage. I found that other tree growers would have some article of clothing for their crew members. During the months between sales, I knit caps for my crew to wear. This accomplished two needs, the workers were easily identifiable out in the field with their bright red caps, and the caps kept the pine needles and sap out of their hair.

Several of the workers had friendly attitudes, which meant I used those particular workers to accompany a family to their chosen tree. The workers were exceptional in taking pictures, either while the family was cutting the tree, or after when the family was carrying the tree to their car, also in entertaining the children, and developing great rapport with the customers. Over the years I followed the kids' progress, and delighted in the changes and challenges they had. One young man became an actor, one of the girls became a nurse, and another boy became an elementary school teacher.

During the week, not too many customers were out to select a tree until after school was over. It was during one of these quiet periods when I was alone, that a very bossy woman arrived to select her tree. One looked more like a Charlie Brown tree and another was just plain weird, with long three-inch needles on the bottom branches and short fat ones in the middle and the top. From this incident I learned that the customer is always right. She looked at the weird tree from every angle, exclaiming over and over what a lovely "Spruce" tree it was. She didn't want to know that it was a Monterey pine gone wrong. After our little song-and-dance around the tree, I heard myself saying, "Yes, it is a lovely 'Spruce' tree." I cut her tree, loaded it into her car, and she drove off happy knowing she had purchased a lovely "Spruce" tree.

Those were the years that I learned that if you have the right attitude, have fun doing something you like to do, and associate with people who are kind and warm (and all tree growers are), your life will be the same. Be good to your employees, and family. Find friends you can count on. Find the humor in your work. Life is what you make of it.

~ KAY STARR
Tree Grower

TUPPERWARE AND TODDLERS

By the time I gave birth to my first child, I was over thirty. Although I knew this would be a life-changing event, for me there were two immediate realizations. One, even though I had always loved my job, I definitely did not want to return to work and let someone else benefit from the daily miracles my little son offered. Two, I did not own one piece of plastic.

My mother told me that I did not need to give up my love of Waterford crystal and Lenox china, but it was imperative that I attend a Tupperware Party. My first party was an awakening. Who knew? Not only did Tupperware offer plates, bowls, and plastic cups, but career opportunities.

I immediately signed up to sell Tupperware. It only made sense to get a representative's discount as I was purchasing so much. Within a year I had worked my way up to being a manager. As a Tupperware manager I was given a company car and able to earn a good living while working from my home.

During the next three years I enjoyed the benefits of a successful business and the special, irreplaceable moments with my son. We also had an endless supply of plastic.

~ LYN R. WHITE
Insurance Agent, www.lwhiteinsurance.com

✦ ✦ ✦

Devote today to something so daring even you can't believe you're doing it.

~ OPRAH WINFREY

What I Didn't Expect to Learn in Cancer School: How to "Be" in Business!

Ahhh! . . . the lessons to be learned in school. I didn't sign up for this unlikely school, but instead, circumstances enrolled me in this penalty, traffic-like school.

What law did I break to deserve cancer, this life or death experience? I think I broke *The Law of Being True to Yourself* and needed a wake-up call. I think I needed to experience some kind of wreckage of my physical body to wake up, open my eyes, mind, and heart. I had long ignored signals that I wasn't being true to me. I lived for and did for everyone else except for me. Being true to me? What exactly did that mean?

Prior to "Cancer School" I obeyed all the signs and rules of the road of daily living. Fully aware of my intelligence, creativity, talents, and hard work, I was equally aware of how often I held back, sabotaged, severely judged, and undervalued myself. Then my life literally came to a screeching halt when my doctor diagnosed cancer. I had heard that repressed anger caused cancer. Thus I embarked on my inward journey, with mentors and spiritual healing help, to find out exactly what fueled this disease. Going back to one of my childhood stories and digging deeper into interpreting its meaning and message for me provided the healing I needed to eliminate the emotional cause of this cancer.

I come from a family of five girls and one boy. I'm the second child. My parents wanted a boy so badly they kept on having girls until my brother, the last child, was born. After each child, the doctors warned my parents of the increasing danger of pregnancy on a health condition that could threaten my mother's life. Immediately after the birth of my brother, the doctors performed a hysterectomy, ending my mother's baby-making career. In my child's mind, I interpreted this to mean that "*females had no value.*" Once we discovered this debilitating belief, all the self-sabotage, self-judgment, and undervaluing myself made sense. No longer wanting to live this way, I healed this interpretation of my past, created a new belief, and created a new life as a female who had incredible value to herself and her world.

Right out of surgery and stepping into this new life, I answered the question, "What do I really want to do with my life right now (besides love and enjoy my family)?" My priorities? Only three things came to mind: 1. Finish writing my book; 2. Finish my visualization CD; and 3. Revisit Italy!

It's interesting to note that the top two were business oriented—business with a passion. I made a priority of *expressing my value* through a book and CD, and by forming a business "*Helping Women Feel and Live Their Value.*"

The book has been ten years in the making—with four versions and thirty rejections! Cancer helped me see the urgency of achieving my dreams. It also helped eliminate or lessen many of my fears of screwing up, being good enough to be an author, having a "voice," being in the media, etc. Nothing in my life about me has been more fearful than cancer. If I can get through that, I can get through ANYTHING.

The book has now been delivered to the publisher, I'm working with a voice coach to produce a higher quality of voice and expression to reproduce the CD, and Italy was simply grand!

I handled the emotional cause and repercussions of cancer and opted to have surgery. Now cancer-free, this is what I learned in how to "be" in business and in life:

The slow lane:

- Simply "shift gears" to living life as if you didn't have many tomorrows
- Become crystal clear on your destination
- Make course adjustments as needed
- Pay attention

The fast lane:

All of the above, plus:

- Acknowledge your magnificent self and just know how valuable you are, worth living a life you absolutely love
- Life is too short, live your dreams NOW
- Go for it! What do you have to lose?
- Put your fears or worries into perspective. Example—Cancer and its effects on my life vs. "Will I look foolish?" "Will people buy my book?" etc. (fears and worries melt away)
- Answer and act on: "What am I willing to die for?"
- "Is my passion, my true path, built into my business?"

People are attracted to passion and value. They will pay more for it. Abundance surrounds those who value themselves enough to *receive* it. Bottom line, BE your highest and best self and do whatever it takes to discover, feel, and live your value. Then watch the increase in your fulfillment . . . and income.

~ MARIA CARTER
Author of Fall In Love With Your Life®
Full version of this story posted at www.FallInLoveWithYourLife.com

Business Builders

AUTHENTIC CONNECTIONS
KNOW NO BOUNDARIES

*J*was born and raised in Manizáles, a colorful town located at the ridge of the Andes Mountains of South America in Colombia. Twenty years ago I left my home and found a new home in the United States. My brother and I were raised with different expectations. For instance, I had a curfew, while my brother didn't. It was also acceptable for him to flirt or even date more than one girl at a time; but as a young woman, that kind of behavior was not accepted. Even though our parents always tried to be fair, the society itself was in charge of marking the differences. Fortunately, I learned to discern those differences, growing up to be the strong woman I am today and conscious of the importance of connecting in my life and in my business. When I was asked to share my story, I identified four clear points that have taken my business to the next level:

1. Look for organizations that support authentic connections.
2. Get inspired, motivated, and charged!
3. Be connected without being over committed.
4. Hire a business coach who understands the value of authentic connections.

As you read on, I challenge you to look at how you are spending your time and with whom you are spending it.

Look for Organizations that
Support Authentic Connections

Networking has been and still is part of my business plan. In the beginning, I learned not every group could fulfill your needs. Because

210 ◆ HEART OF A WOMAN IN BUSINESS

I look to connect with other women who have similar values and will help my business and self grow, I have participated in various women's groups. The synergy, energy, and the ability to form authentic connections are unbelievable. At some of these meetings, I have had the opportunity to mentor and connect with the woman seated next to me. Based on the questions asked, some have given me great suggestions regarding challenging situations that I was dealing with at the time. Through these relationships, I also found accountability and invaluable friendships. While I was attending a group coaching program several years ago, I exchanged e-mails with a senior sales director from Mary Kay. We held each other accountable for our goals for an entire month. There is no doubt about it—many authentic connections happen in womens' networking groups!

In 2004, I joined a service organization called Soroptimist International; in 2007 I became club president. The minute I found out their slogan was *"Best for Women,"* I wanted to be part of it. Soroptimists has helped me grow both personally and professionally. We are proud to be professional businesswomen helping women and girls in the community and throughout the world. Connecting with other women who share your values will dramatically impact you as an individual and as a woman in business.

Get Inspired, Motivated, and Charged!

What is it that inspires you? Is it money, recognition, volunteering, self-satisfaction, interactivity, spirituality, or maybe freedom? Write down what it is that inspires you to be in business for yourself. Refer to this when you feel frustrated and anxious because things aren't going as planned in your business, and it will keep you on track and inspired.

My motivation in business is linked to authentic connections, freedom, and self-satisfaction. It is an awesome feeling when I find someone who willingly shares experiences, knowledge, and business contacts without hesitation. What's even better is when our authentic conversations include fashion, business, politics, and even labor pains. I am in awe when I see a woman fearlessly go up on stage and speak from her heart, sharing her deepest thoughts and feelings. I am inspired, and I immediately identify that woman as a genuine connector!

One of the advantages of being our own bosses is the freedom to schedule our time. We can get up when we please, or we can take off on a short vacation without asking anyone. Time management was one of the most difficult obstacles to bypass when I started my business. I have learned to have a "To Do List" and prioritize my jobs according to due dates and involvement. I mark items off the list as I complete them, and every evening, I make my list for the next day. Give yourself cushion time to complete any task and tell your customer that it will take you five days when in reality you can have it completed in two days. One of my coaches used to say, *"Under promise and over deliver!"* That is the best way to avoid stress and unnecessary headaches, plus you will develop customers for life.

Self-satisfaction is another inspiration in business. Be passionate about what you do and be proud of the work you deliver, and you will see how soon your clientele multiplies.

Be Connected Without Being Overcommitted

I am a volunteer by nature, and I know many of you are as well. If you do not have a large budget for advertising, offering your time and skills at key events will give you and your business excellent exposure.

Regularly attending organizations that you belong to will make you visible so clients can identify you, what you do, and how you can help them. Volunteering gives you the opportunity to make important connections and build your sphere of influence. The greatest lesson I have learned through volunteering is sometimes you need to say no in order to continue to move your business forward.

I have grown my business based on networking and referrals, especially through connections with other women, but while finding customers is not difficult, keeping them is a challenge due to the competition around you. How do I keep my customers? I thrive in customer service. In December of 2006, I was presented the "Excellence in the Service Industry Award." Receiving the award allowed me to reflect on the amount of time I have dedicated to numerous organizations over the years. I have proven efficiency, organization, professionalism, and excellent work, but I constantly have to control the time that I dedicate to offer my services for free.

Carefully planning your time will allow you to avoid stress, take care of your customers, and make time for volunteering. It is also important to thoughtfully plan your volunteer time. Examine the groups you are currently involved with and count the number of hours you are volunteering. It is up to you to know how far you can go with it and you are the only person who can say no. Have a weekly calendar, with a limit each week, so next time someone calls for a "freebie," be honest and politely decline. If it is something you want to do, determine what the consequences might be of accepting the assignment. The bottom line is to always refer back to your values and what is most important to you and the mission of your business.

Hire a Business Coach who Understands
the Value of Authentic Connections

Several years ago, I made an instant connection at a Chamber of Commerce meeting with another businesswoman. I openly shared with her my business and personal challenges. She was a good listener and often told others of my business talents. I felt comfortable around her and decided to hire her as my business coach. One of the things we worked on was my inability to say, "No." My business was suffering the consequences of spending 75 percent of my time volunteering. Through coaching, she helped me create a more balanced life, giving more time to myself and my family while still being productive.

I hired another business coach many years later. While she has a different style of coaching, she understands the power of making authentic connections and focuses on my need to be intentional. After every session, I believe I am capable of doing anything I set my mind out to do. My business has grown tremendously, and I am now launching a second company.

Because it's easy to become absorbed by the day-to-day operational issues of the business, I recommend hiring a business coach to help you remain focused, increase productivity and profits, and remind you of the importance of living an authentic life.

These four tips will help you grow your business because making connections is part of life. When we connect, it feels right, it's comfortable and it fits, like a piece of a puzzle. Authentic connections know no boundaries. Stay open to the possibilities because you never know when you will make an authentic connection.

~ MARCY DECATO
Creative Solutions Marketing, LLC, www.cswebsitedesign.com

DEVELOP A POSITIVE BELIEF
ABOUT SELF-PROMOTION

*S*elf-promotion, when done effectively, works for any business or career. Once you begin to implement the proven marketing strategies behind it . . . it's easy to be successful in anything you set your mind to. In fact, when you promote yourself over and over again, you will begin to enjoy it more, and it will reward you many times over in return.

I shockingly discovered that an average of 87 percent of the thousands of business people I've surveyed did not feel comfortable promoting themselves and avoided it most of the time.

In business we understand that if we don't promote and market we can't be successful. Right? No matter how great your service is or what amazing value you offer, if prospects don't know about you, you're not going to win the opportunity to do business with them.

Therefore, if you don't promote yourself . . . it goes against the grain of all sales and marketing success! Right?

Why do so many people feel uncomfortable with self-promotion? Perhaps it's because much of what they believe to be true about self-promotion comes from past programming that dates back to their childhood. When you grew up you may have heard comments like this, "It's not polite to talk about yourself. It will come across as pushy or rude."

Too many of us have ten, twenty, thirty, or more years of negative and/or limited beliefs rattling around in our heads about the concept of self-promotion. These limiting and negative beliefs have been programmed into our subconscious minds for years.

What were your parents, teachers, or guardians like when you were growing up? Did they believe in promoting themselves? Did they promote your self-esteem to believe that you could do anything you set your mind to? Were they risk-takers or were they conservative?

We usually hate to admit it, but we are all creatures of habit, especially when habits have been programmed into our brains since childhood.

Some people are so conditioned against self-promotion they are closed minded about it; no matter how much it might benefit them. Now, I don't expect you to change your belief overnight, but you can start by opening your mind to believing differently about self-promotion from this day forward.

Why believe differently? Because you can't be truly successful if you aren't willing to let people know that you, your product, and/or services exist. If you aren't willing to promote your talents, expertise, and products, others will quickly pass you by. The world is not going to beat a path to your door unless you pave the way.

Resenting self-promotion is one of the greatest obstacles to success. *If you don't toot your own horn, you can't enjoy the music.*

~ DEBBIE ALLEN
International Business Speaker, Author of Skyrocketing Sales, *www.DebbieAllen.com*

✦ ✦ ✦

In every community, there is work to be done. In every nation, there are wounds to heal. In every heart, there is the power to do it.

~ MARIANNE WILLIAMSON
Author of A Woman's Worth

GET A NEW ATTITUDE
WHEN IT COMES TO SALES

*W*hy is it that you, as a business owner, are willing to do anything it takes to grow your business—except sales? Since the reality is, a business cannot grow (not to mention exist) without sales, why do most entrepreneurs tend to overlook this aspect when planning their businesses? Why do you want to give away 10 percent of your profits by hiring a sales person when you can do it yourself?

It could be that selling can sometimes seem like a form of confrontation, which explains why you find the process difficult or nerve-wracking. If you were to substitute positive expectations of success, for negative fears of failure then selling could very well become an enjoyable experience. Another hurdle comes when your passion is no longer a "hobby," and it turns into "pressure to perform" when a "price" is now attached for the service.

Selling simply involves relationships with people. Your sale may be solving a client problem, or changing the status quo of how they do business; but on the other side of that sale is still a *person*. Basically, people do business with people they like, or more importantly, with people they trust.

In reality, you have been selling since you could talk. Think back to how you would sell your idea to your friends of going to one movie over another; or how you negotiated with your parents to stay out past your normal curfew; or how you felt when you were paid for a paper route, babysitting service, or weekly chores. Guess what—you were selling! See, it's not hard to do. When you remove the fear factor, it comes down to *can* you sell, and *will* you sell.

Here are three key points to remember when it comes to sales:
1. Selling is about attitude and values.
2. Selling is relationships with people.
3. Selling is an art and a science.

#1 Selling Is About Attitudes and Values
Our attitude towards life determines
life's attitude towards us.
~ EARL NIGHTINGALE

The idea of *congruence* was developed by a company called Integrity Solutions®. This system helps you to create a harmonic balance of the following five areas of selling:

- **Define your view of selling:** Selling is easier when you believe that selling is a noble profession that identifies and satisfies people's needs; and creates value for them.
- **Review your abilities:** Once you understand what selling is, you believe that you have the necessary talents and abilities to be successful doing it. (Remember you have been doing this since you could talk!)
- **Believe in your product:** You must believe that your product or service will create value for people over and above the cost.
- **Commit to action:** You understand the activities necessary for success and commit to diligently doing them on a regular basis.
- **Assess your value system:** You possess a high degree of internal sincerity, purpose, and integrity that drives your behavior.

If you are not confident in any of these areas, you will not feel congruent, or in harmony, thus your attitude can be negatively affected.

#2 Selling is Relationships With People
Professional Sales Credo: You can have everything in life that you want, if you will just help enough people get what they want.
~ ZIG ZIGLAR

Too often we choose a selling model that is not congruent with who we are, which makes us more uncomfortable with the selling side of the business. The traditional sales model pushes one to "create" a need in order to make the sale. The newer relationship selling model is based on "defining" a need, which then produces a consultive sales approach to the client's problem. So choose a model that fits you!

In the relationship model, your value system is important to understand. There is an assessment that will help you to define your value system, as well as learn how to identify your client's value system. This helps you understand how your prospective clients view the world, review information, make decisions, or even handle stress. The more you are able to adjust your behavior to make your client comfortable with you, the more successful you will be in sales.

#3 Selling is an Art and a Science
You may not have chosen sales as a profession, it may have chosen you . . . either way, learn to sell on purpose.
~ CHRIS LYTLE
The Accidental Salesperson

Whether you are an "accidental salesperson" or not, it is important to recognize that sales is both an art and a science. It is an art, in that it is one of the most creative aspects of your business. The ability to define the clients needs, to help them to assess their current status quo, to work within their budgetary parameters; to basically make a sale work for everyone involves the creative thinking process to problem solving.

The science aspect of sales involves those learned, committed action steps noted in #1 that are the logical sequences of events that produce the sale and retains the client. This is the back end work from filling the sales pipeline (or prospecting), to following up, to the presentation of the proposal of work, to the commitment to a contractual agreement, to the producing of the service or product that you promised the client, to the ongoing customer relationship management . . . the entire sales process of committed action steps.

So in conclusion, you are your best salesperson. You will need to develop the sales system for your company that is congruent with your company image, with your product and service, and with your marketing strategies. So try reducing your own fear of selling first, before you give away 10 percent of your profit.

~ MICHELLE BURKART
President of TH!NKbusiness, www.think-biz.com

♦ ♦ ♦

What you are is God's gift to you.
What you become is your gift to God.
~ ELEANOR ROOSEVELT

SECRETS TO BECOMING A
MASTER SALES COMMUNICATOR

Knowing how to effectively communicate is essential for any person to become successful in sales. The purpose of communication is to get your message across to your prospects in the best way possible. Good communication takes skill, since messages can often become misinterpreted by one or more of the parties involved. When this happens it causes unnecessary confusion and moves you further away from connecting to your prospect.

Your communication is successful only when both the sender and the receiver perceive it in the same way. By successfully getting your message across, you convey your thoughts and ideas effectively. When not successful, the thoughts and ideas that you convey do not necessarily reflect your own, causing a communication breakdown. This breakdown can cause you to lose trust and belief in your prospect.

To communicate effectively, you must clearly understand what your core message is, and how your prospect will perceive your message. Communication breakdown can pop up at every stage of the sale, causing you to lose out on many sales opportunities. Therefore, to become a more effective communicator and get your point across without misunderstanding and confusion, your goal should be to lessen the frequency of communication breakdown at each stage of the process with clear, concise, accurate, well-planned communication.

Stage #1: To establish yourself as a master sales communicator you must first establish credibility with your prospect. This involves displaying knowledge of the subject, your prospect, and the context in which your message is delivered.

Stage #2: Consider the message itself. Written, oral, and nonverbal communications all are affected by your tone, your individual communication style of communication, what you leave in and what you leave out of the conversation. How you communicate both verbally and in writing is very important to how your prospect perceives your point of view. What you want your message to do is to motivate and inspire your prospects into taking action and buying from you.

Stage #3: Consider how best to communicate with your prospect. You may choose to communicate verbally in person, by telephone, e-mail, letters, greeting cards, etc.

Stage #4: Keep in mind the actions or reactions you hope your message prompts in your prospect. Keep in mind too, that your prospect also enters into the conversation with his or her own communication style. Their communication will include new ideas, feelings, and emotions that will undoubtedly influence how they understand and relate to your message, and also how they respond. To be a master sales communicator, you must consider these possible responses before delivering your message. This will allow you to be prepared and ready to respond with the appropriate communication skills.

Stage #5: Your prospect will provide you with personal feedback, verbal, and nonverbal reactions to your communicated message. To deliver your message effectively, you must commit to breaking down the barriers that exist in each of these stages of the communication process. If your message is too lengthy, disorganized, or contains incorrect information about your products or services, you can expect to be misunderstood. Also, the use of ineffective body language that confuses the message or shows your lack of confidence will also allow you to disconnect with your prospect.

Don't offer too much information too soon. When in doubt, less is oftentimes more. Remember to listen more and communicate less verbally when you begin a conversation with a new prospect. Be respectful of your prospect's time, and keep their interests and concerns in the forefront.

Once you understand how these five stages work and start to implement them into your sale's message, you will soon discover your communication skills improving.

~ DEBBIE ALLEN
International Business Speaker, Author of Skyrocketing Sales, *www.DebbieAllen.com*

Hunch. Gut feeling. Voice of God. Instinct. Many names. One Force.
~ CATH KACHUR-DESTEFANO

We can do no great things, only small things with great love.
~ MOTHER TERESA

The future belongs to those who believe in the beauty of their dreams.
~ ELEANOR ROOSEVELT

Woman once made equal to man become his superior.
~ SOCRATES

Nurturing Our Mind, Body, & Spirit

NURTURE YOURSELF
AND KEEP YOUR SANITY

*H*ere are four simple ways to help keep balance in your daily life, so you are able to be there for yourself, your children, and loved ones. According to stress management experts, we have four support systems available that offer us unconditional love and support.

Pets

Pets are nonjudgmental, forgiving, sensitive, and supportive. They instinctively know when we need a hug or are feeling emotional, depressed, and upset, and don't run at the first sign of tears! Medical research even proves that hugging a pet lowers blood pressure, and helps to rebuild the immune system.

Faith—Spiritual Belief System

This inner compass enables us bring forth that wisdom, authenticity, and insight into all we do on a daily basis. These beliefs center our moral foundation, offering direction, and trust to walk to our path in this world.

Passion Hobbies

Passion hobbies are pastimes that nurture our spirit and balance our lives. Reading; walking, dancing, running, aerobics or exercise; crafts; puzzles; playing with kids; or shopping!

Special People

These may be relatives, or significant others, still be living, or have already made their transition. They are highly supportive kindred spirits. We can pick up conversations with them, right where we left off, without missing a beat.

You have numerous gifts to give to the world today— and those gifts are needed. Nurture yourself first, and those challenges become easier to handle, with less stress, greater peace and calm. Utilize these unconditional support systems to bring you more balance and joy in your daily life.

~ SHERYL ROUSH
Speaker, author of Sparkle-Tudes! *and* Heart of a Woman
www.SparklePresentations.com

✦ ✦ ✦

You can be certain that what you fear is in control of your life.
~ MOONSTONE STAR WHITE
www.SpiritWindPublishing.com

The world is terrified by joyful women. Take a stand—be one anyway!
~ MARIANNE WILLIAMSON
Author of A Return to Love

Breathe. Let go. And remind yourself that this very moment is the only one you know you have for sure.
~ OPRAH WINFREY

Rejuvenating the Heart of
a Success-Oriented Woman

*W*hen you're a hard working woman in today's culture, chances you give a lot more than you receive, you often put your self-care secondary, and you are exhausted. I empathize with you, as rejuvenating oneself is an ongoing challenge I have been managing for years. When I was in the corporate world, I used to go outside to the luxury hotel next door or drive to a local park. I would sit out by the pool or trees and pretend I was on vacation for twenty minutes of my lunch break. Getting outside regularly is a great way to get your vitamin D replenished from the sun. If it is cold outside, ten minutes is all you need.

Some offices are instituting meditation rooms. If you are in management or have a manager, discuss the possibility of providing a room where you can light it with soft lighting, have some plants and some chairs and/or pillows for meditating. A sofa and CD player would be great options as well. Warm colors and pictures of nature on the walls would help. A little Zen clock with a timer would be helpful to ensure people don't fall asleep there.

The mind is a powerful entity. When we give it some quiet time, amazing things can happen. As a hypnotherapist, I have created custom visualization CDs for people that have helped them stop stuttering, be more relaxed, focused, productive, and athletic. They have relieved pain and anxiety as well as shed pounds. I encourage you to find the time to take a power nap. It involves twenty minutes where you either meditate, use a guided relaxation program, or nap.

If you would like to try a guided relaxation audio, there is a free fifteen-minute audio available at *www.ReEnergizenow.com.* Load this onto your MP3 player and take your mini-vacation at the office any time you need a break. You can use this during that low energy time of day. You'd be amazed at what a power nap can do for you. Often times these guided relaxation audios have versions to which you can fall asleep; there is a nice selection of these power-napping audios at *www.SanDiegoHypnosisWorks.com.*

If you really have a lot going on, you may be in need of more rest. Most women today do not get enough rest. If this has been a pattern for a while, work on getting eight to nine hours of sleep daily.

Furthermore, make a list of ways to nurture yourself and do one thing a day. Here are some additional ideas for your list: meditate, gentle yoga class, receive a massage, take a bath, float, drink more water, take conscious breaths during your day, take a nap, sleep, take a day off and do nothing, get a facial or give yourself a facial, go for a walk, go for tea with a girlfriend, hire a babysitter and go to a movie, journal, slow down, keep relaxing music on in the evening, write a love letter to yourself, ask for a hug from someone close you, take a vacation or staycation (vacation at home), read the other inspiring books, such as *Heart* books by Sheryl Roush (*www.HeartBookSeries. com*), develop close relationships with like-minded women or join communities of women who will celebrate and inspire you, like Club Joy at *www.WomenInJoy.com.*

Most of all I want to remind you of the incredible woman you are. You are precious and lovable and deserve the very best that life has to offer. So love yourself a lot. Think about how you would treat your best friend whom you adore. Would you buy her gifts, say great things about her, be there for her to listen to her deepest thoughts and feelings? Yes, you would—so do that for yourself.

Rejuvenation is an ongoing process. Radical self-care pays off. You will look younger, be more productive, and thus be able to work less. You are reading this because your health needs to be a greater priority. That doesn't just mean exercising and eating right. It means rest, relaxation, and nurturing.

Here's to your joy and rejuvenation.

~ LAURA RUBINSTEIN
Certified Hypnotherapist and Master Leadership Coach
www.TransformYourBody.com

◆ ◆ ◆

WHAT INSPIRES YOU?

What inspires you?
Who are your inspirations (based on your passion, values, and beliefs)?
Which places and things inspire you?

Now find ways to incorporate these people, places, things, and moments into your daily life. This is one of the key components in establishing sustainability. Learn how to put the guilt aside so you can allow for these vital components that nurture you to grow.

~ LIZ MYERS, M.A.
Rooted Living Coaching, www.RootedLiving.com

TAKE A BREAK!

*S*et your project(s) aside—take a break—and refresh your mind, body, and spirit! Moving to a new location and changing your scenery, even when done in short intervals, can take you out of a stuck place and renew your perspective. Pausing for refreshment time will serve your project(s) well and bring you more peace. Stimulate your creativity and productivity with these ideas:

Enjoy lunch outside. Turn your phones off and take a few moments to listen to the call of the songbirds. Feel the breeze lift your spirits. Renew your energy.

Take morning and afternoon breaks (five to ten minutes each) and enjoy the peaceful sanctuary of your "outdoor home." A few minutes to breathe in the fresh air and place the stale "challenges" on pause can renew your perspective and revitalize your spirit.

Walk around the block for a fresh start. Find the closest park bench and sit still for a few moments.

Go to the closest grassy area and sit down. Connect with the sacred earth. If you feel comfortable doing so, close and rest your eyes for a while. Release any thoughts of work during this time. Focus instead on any nature sounds, i.e. the birds or the wind.

Go to an outdoor café or coffee house for your lunch break. Breathe out any pent up concerns from the office and breathe in the new life within your change of scenery.

If you're near a fountain or a quiet nook, allow yourself a pause at one of these refreshment centers to recharge your mind, body, spirit, and soul. You'll feel more alive when you return to your desk.

You deserve this time for rejuvenation. You'll be more motivated to jump back into your projects when you return. Your creative expression and energized spirit will thank you. Are you ready to accomplish another sensational project? Take a break!

~ SUZAN TUSSON, CPCC
Author, Award-winning Author and Certified Life Coach, http://wisewithin.wordpress.com
© 2008 by Suzan Tusson-McNeil

✦ ✦ ✦

KEEPING YOUR BALANCE

Although it really does feel like you are at the mercy of other people's emotions, you can stay in an energy that serves you best. You don't have to get on the emotional roller coaster with them. When you allow yourself to become more of an observer in any given situation you free yourself from believing you are being personally attacked or that you need to solve their stuff. It helps you remember they are speaking from their truth and it doesn't necessarily represent your truth. When you know who you are, how you want to feel, and that you really do want the highest good for all involved, you create an energetic vibration that can move from you to them, ultimately changing the outcome of any situation allowing you to walk away feeling good that you stayed connected to your energy.

~ LINDA SALAZAR
Certified Personal Life Coach, Author, Speaker, www.AwakenTheGenieWithin.com
© 2005 Linda Salazar

SPARKLE-TUDE™ BOOSTERS

*T*oday, we need little attitude "boosters" to help us overcome negative thoughts and actions that so easily creep into our daily lives. We were born with passion, a natural zest for life, curiosity, playfulness, and grace. These Sparkle-Tudes™ help us rejuvenate that unbridled excitement, spirit, and joyful expression:

Start off the day on a positive tone. How we wake up in the morning sets the pace for the rest of our day.

Have only positive thoughts toward yourself and others. Carefully guard your thoughts. Attitude, or our truest belief about things, is that highly powered magnet that either attracts—or repels! Life is composed of our moment-by-moment thoughts.

Look for the good in yourself and others. The universal principle is that whatever thoughts we have about other people, these are also true of ourselves, as we are all connected, and we are all one. What we see in others are reflections of ourselves.

Believe in yourself, your talents, and your unique gifts. You were given significant strengths, and have developed skills to support those—use them!

Don't take things "personally." Let it go and move on!

Affirm a daily spirit of gratitude. Start off the day with positive affirmations and anticipations of the day. I say, "Thank you God, for the gift of this glorious day. I rise, rejoice, and am glad in it. Thank you for every way in which I experience your love. I give thanks that my every thought, word, and act is only loving and supportive." End the day summarizing the blessings you received.

Use unconditional support systems to keep your balance, perspective and sanity: Pets, faith, passion hobbies, and special people.

~ SHERYL ROUSH
Speaker, author of Sparkle-Tudes!™ *and* Heart of A Woman, *www.HeartBookSeries.com*

◆ ◆ ◆

AFFIRMATIONS FOR HONORING OURSELVES

I am a valued human being.
I am always treated with respect.
I am empowered.
I am supportive of other women.
I easily speak up for myself.
I deserve to have boundaries.
My boundaries are respected.
I make waves whenever I need to.
I have a good support team.
I have integrity.
The more open I am, the safer I am.
I am a woman healing other women.
I have a strong energy barrier.
The men in my life honor women.
I take my power back. I love and honor myself.

~ LOUISE L. HAY
Author of Empowering Women

20 Ways to be Wealthier and Healthier

1. Develop three attitudes daily:
   a. "I like me" attitude
   b. "I like you" attitude
   c. "I improve me" attitude
2. Take a regular inventory in the six areas of your life: Physical, Mental, Spiritual, Social, Financial, and Family.
3. Get physical—begin a walking program.
4. Develop your inner self—practice meditation, prayer, and introspection.
5. Laugh every day—it is internal jogging.
6. Build positive personality traits—enthusiasm—self-confidence.
7. Get organized at home and at work.
8. Train your mind to see and accept opportunities.
9. Increase your learning—read and listen more.
10. Express yourself—reach out and touch.
11. Set priorities—personally and professionally.
12. Increase productivity—not activity.
13. Reward yourself.
14. Put yourself in the other person's shoes.
15. Give others RAP (recognition, appreciation, praise).
16. Balance your emotions with logic—use both sides of the brain.
17. Get involved in something you believe in.
18. Take charge of your life: "I am in charge of me with God's help."
19. Be thankful in all things.
20. You become what you think—so think what you become.

~ Dr. Zonnya
The First Lady of Motivation, Speaker, Author, www.drzonnya.org

HOW TO SAVOR A HEALTHY LIFE

*B*usiness and money seem to take a front seat in our lives as the pressures of "making a living," paying the bills, and getting ahead demand the most fuel. Why do we want money anyway? Usually it represents freedom—freedom to do what you want, when you want, with whom you want. Freedom to buy what you want, live where you want, to give to charities of your choice, to serve others how and when you want.

Freedom should not come at the cost of your health. You cannot store fitness as you can store money in a savings account. You must take care of your health daily.

Some people focus on making money at the expense of their health. They gain weight because they don't eat right and they don't exercise and are sedentary. Relaxation is in front of a television or movie screen, once again a sedentary activity. They don't get enough sleep or they pop pills to stay awake.

It's simple to write about savoring a healthy life and much harder to do. You have to break habits, try new ways of doing things, eat different food and yes, even exercise! Just do one at a time, so that you do not become overwhelmed.

Tips to savor a healthy life:

- *Eat less and chew more.*
- *Eat more fruit and vegetables.*
- *Eat according to your activity level. A long hike will need more food energy.*
- *Find a simple exercise routine at home or at the gym.*
- *Make contact with another person such as massage or simply holding hands.*

- *Relax by taking a walk instead of watching TV.*
- *Give love and recognition with kind words and silent gestures such as a smile.*
- *Do activities with and for another person as a present by "being present" for them.*
- *Clean up your lifestyle: your home, your environment; create a clean state of mind.*
- *Appreciate, appreciate, appreciate.*

~ SHERRIE ROSE
www.SavorHealthyLife.com

✦ ✦ ✦

Do not go where the path may lead; go instead where there is no path and leave a trail.
~ RALPH WALDO EMERSON

God gave women intuition and femininity. Used properly, the combination easily jumbles the brain of any man I've ever met.
~ FARRAH FAWCETT

Always be a first-rate version of yourself, instead of a second-rate version of somebody else.
~ JUDY GARLAND

Exercise:
Developing a Livable Routine

Ready to give up the "all or nothing" self-defeating exercise pattern? You know, the rigorous, all out, going for broke exercise for two months then recover from it with the couch potato syndrome for the next year and a half. Here's a technique that you can easily maintain throughout your life.

First, set a *minimum* amount of exercise—a goal that is reachable under *any* circumstances. If you have to work twenty extra hours that week, and your house flooded and the babysitter quit, ask yourself how much exercise could you do under these extreme situations. Five minutes once per week is sufficient. Although it is not enough to accomplish any real fitness, this is not the first goal. *Developing success and a livable routine that you can maintain over time is the first goal.* Of course, those who are accustomed to more of a disciplined pattern may set their minimum goal as once per week for twenty minutes or twice per week for ten minutes each time. Remember, choose a pattern you can do under almost any of life's demands.

Next, set a *maximum* amount of weekly exercise. This is to prevent burnout. It is crucial that you don't exceed your maximum if you are to change the sabotage associated with "all or nothing" patterns. Your maximum should be sufficient to get you reasonably healthy. You should determine an amount you can manage under average life circumstances. I like to use the President John F. Kennedy's guidelines, twenty to thirty minutes, three times per week.

Studies show this low level exercise is enough to affect longevity, general health, and risk of heart disease or stroke. Since twenty minutes, three times per week is enough to do the job, why then, unless you really enjoy exercise or have goals for athletic achievement would you demand that you exercise more? Now that you know excessive exercise is not necessary, can you relax with it?

Now accept the minimum and maximum routines as your overall pattern. There will be weeks in which, for what ever reason, you will not do more than your minimum. Because you will feel good about reaching your goal, even at its minimum, you will stay motivated to reach your higher goals.

There are biorhythms in life. Some days you have more energy than others. Some weeks life hands you more problems than others. When you allow for these differences by being flexible with your expectations, you will be successful. When you are successful, you are motivated to continue. Now isn't this better than the "all or nothing" which put you at the top for a couple of months and then at the bottom for years?

~ DR. NIKKI GOLDMAN
Author, www.DrNikkiGoldman.com
Excerpt from Success for the Diet Dropout: Proven Life Strategies for Women Who Want to Stop Hating Their Bodies

✦ ✦ ✦

ADVICE TO WOMEN

Learn to love being alone with yourself.
Do something by yourself each month . . .
go for a hike, make a picnic, see a movie,
or take a weekend away.
Fall in love and become friends with you as a person.
Don't be afraid to feel and experience the depths of loneliness.
Only then can you discover your true strength and soul.

~ IVKA ADAM

PRACTICE YOGA TO
PROMOTE HEALTH WEALTH

*W*e've all heard the saying, "Without your health, you have nothing." Yoga is one of the simplest forms of exercise that may also include meditation and is a great way to stay healthy. There are a variety of yoga practices each with names harder to spell and pronounce than the next.

A popular form of yoga, Hatha Yoga, focuses on poses and posture. The great thing about yoga is that you have to be in the now, in the moment, or you will simply fall over. It is a wonderful concentration to link the mind and body.

Another form of yoga, Kundalini Yoga, is often done with your eyes closed. Kundalini is a Sanskrit word that means "coiled up" or "coiling like a snake." Kundalini Yoga focuses on moving the coiled up energy in your body and releasing it.

Yoga usually only requires a yoga mat and even they are optional. You can do yoga at home by watching DVD's or listening to audio CD's that walk you through the movements. I prefer a yoga class since there is a group energy with people focusing together, which feels very supportive.

One of my favorite forms of yoga is Crystal Bowl Yoga. Using crystal bowls, often known as Tibetan Singing Bowls, during the yoga postures or while in resting poses, energy is moved with the use of sound. The vibrations emanating from the crystal bowls positively affects the water in our bodies. Physically we are made up of water, about 60 to 65 percent for men and 50 to 60 percent for women. The human brain is about 85 percent water and our bones are between 10 to 15 percent water. The chemical structure of water, H_2O, gives it the ability to disassemble and rearrange other molecules essential to the chemistry of life. In short, sound moves us.

In addition to the physical benefits of yoga, there is the benefit of a peaceful state of mind. "Wealthy is the man (or woman) who has a peace of mind." With peace of mind you focus on your higher pursuit which may be the business of accumulating material wealth. The practice of yoga will promote both health and wealth.

~ SHERRIE ROSE
www.PromoteHealthWealth.com

✦ ✦ ✦

Ask for what you want and be prepared to get it.
~ MAYA ANGELOU
Educator, Author, Actor, Activist, Humanitarian

. . . to be loved, happy, not to settle for something less than you deserve.
~ JENNIFER ANISTON

Love yourself first and everything else falls into line. You have to really love yourself to get anything done in this world.
~ LUCILLE BALL

Be courageous. It's one of the only places left uncrowded.
~ ANITA RODDICK

MINDFUL EATING AND ENERGY

Ahhh! I overeat and sabotage my diet! Why do I keep doing this and how to do I get back on track?

Whether you are trying to drop pounds or just maintain your weight, one of the most frustrating challenges can be eating appropriate portions and sticking to your nutrition plan.

You could blame it on lack of knowledge about what to eat and when to eat. Or you could claim that healthy foods just aren't available. Although, both can be valid arguments, if you really take a deeper look, those could be excuses for not sticking to your plan.

So, why do you overeat, even though you've had enough? I asked myself that question when I grabbed a few extra cookies last week at our dinner out in Phoenix. Even though I eat healthy and considered the cookies "a treat," why did I have to have three cookies instead of just having one? These questions can surface not just during vacation, but in everyday life, too. Why do you have double portions, even though you know one is enough? Why are you so afraid of "being hungry" in a culture where food is more widely available than anywhere?

You may imagine that it takes lots of protein, veggies, or extra portions in order to be strong and healthy. But, actually, large quantities of food can tire the system when you overload it, thus impeding your digestive process. And when your system is not able to eliminate properly, illness can occur.

Then, why do you do it? I know for me I often turn to food as a solution to whatever I'm facing. Oh, I'm tired . . . it must be low blood sugar and I need to eat something. Oh, I have a headache . . . I bet some food would take it away. Oh, it's noon . . . I must be hungry. It's lunch time, right?

We live in a society where we turn to food for several of our needs. It ends up being our comfort, our social enjoyment, our reward. You name it, food does it. Think of how early in life this started. What did you get if you succeeded on a test or played a great sports game? I know that I celebrated with Mountain Dew and pepperoni pizza at the local pizza place or trip to the ice cream shop for an extra large treat or the ice cream cone dipped in chocolate. Or for a really big accomplishment it was a Butterfinger Blizzard. Not that any of this is bad; you should celebrate as a kid but, over time, food is continually used to fulfill your needs. After a while you can't separate that home run in your "baseball game and Dairy Queen" with "I feel tired or unsure or stressed, so I want that same comfort and satisfaction." To understand this further, let's dive even deeper about who you really are and why you make the decisions you do.

You have your physical body and your spiritual or "etheric" body. Ideally when you eat, you would savor the food until you are almost full and then stop. You would not continue to eat until you are stuffed, but rather stop when you are slightly hungry. What happens at the point where your body is "almost satisfied" is that your etheric body comes in to fulfill the elements you still need. So, in the end, you feel satisfied for longer. When you eat to the point of fullness or overeat, it actually lowers your energy level, feeding a lower spiritual energy and makes you crave even more. Because those lower energies are extremely powerful, you continue to overeat and actually feel hungrier than before you started. I was a bit confused when I first started learning about the spiritual side to eating. Although it may not make complete sense right now, here's an important point to keep in mind. Have you ever noticed when you eat a lighter meal you have more energy and stamina? Then, think back to that heavy meal where you felt really full. How much energy did you have then? Also, have you ever been curious why after such a big meal, in another hour or so you felt hungry again? How could you be hungry even though you just ate? Why do you want the third or fourth brownie or piece of pizza? Of course, part of the increased cravings can be from lack of nutrition or sugar triggers. But, if you know you are getting the appropriate vitamins and minerals for your body requirements, there may be deeper reasons for your desires. Now comes the big question. What do you do?

Your Action Step

Continue to be mindful of what you are eating and why. Not that you need to analyze at every meal, but if you find yourself grabbing extra snacks or eating to the point of being uncomfortably full, think about what need the food may be fulfilling. Don't judge or criticize, just notice, and then be more mindful next time. Awareness is always the first step in making changes. Also, try to stop eating right before you feel full. Remember if you feel really hungry, you can always eat more later, however, I bet you will find yourself being satisfied for longer.

Why we overeat is a complex question with complex answers. But, it all starts with awareness and remembering that we have the power of choice. The ability to choose differently can be one of the most empowering forces we have.

~ JEANIE CALLEN BARAT
"The Fitness Jeanie," Celebrity Trainer, Founder, Callen Fitness, Inc.
www.TheFitnessJeanie.com and www.Fit2BeMoms.com

STAYING FIT AT THE OFFICE: TURN YOUR DESK INTO A FITNESS CENTER

"*I* don't have time to exercise!" The "E" word may turn you off, but being sedentary should be what scares you. A sedentary lifestyle will shorten your life; a fitness lifestyle will lengthen it. That's why I don't like to call fitness exercise.

You can be fit at any age and any size. Fitness is not about thinness. The number on the scale is not the important number. There is no "normal" weight. There are, however, normal levels for blood pressure, blood sugar, and cholesterol. If these numbers are normal, you are healthy, even if you're a plus-sized woman.

We perceive the "E" word as something we should start doing— tomorrow! In reality, you can be fit everyday without having to lift weights, run a marathon, or ever step foot in a gym. In fact, you can start your fitness regime right now at your desk.

Immobility is your enemy. Fitness is activity—any activity. These routines are designed to get you moving every day. You don't need special equipment, and you don't need special clothes. The best way to remind yourself to do this routine is to schedule it on your Outlook calendar—like a meeting. This entire routine takes fifteen to twenty minutes. Schedule it for two ten-minute breaks. Do the legs and back in the morning and the upper body in the afternoon.

Legs (flats or sneakers are helpful)

1. *Desk Chair Ballet*
   a. Lower your desk chair to put your knees at a right angle.
   b. Sitting with your arms crossed across your chest, use your feet to walk yourself forward. Walk forward for thirty seconds (or until you run out of room!).

    c. Push yourself backwards for thirty seconds or the same distance.

    d. Alternative choreography: if space and safety allow, circle your desk.

    e. Advanced variation: Reach up, fully extending your arms. Bring your arms up and down while moving forward and backward in your chair.

2. *Pop Goes the Weasel*

    a. Find a sturdy chair without wheels (not a folding chair) or back your wheeled desk chair against a wall.

    b. Lower your desk chair to put your knees at a right angle.

    c. Cross your arms across your chest.

    d. Stand up and sit down twenty times in a row.

3. *Desk Drawer Stretchy*

    a. Open your bottom desk drawer. Extend your leg and rest your heel on the open drawer (you might want to use a small towel for comfort under your heel). If your CPU is under your desk, you can rest your leg on that.

    b. Keeping a flat back, stretch over the elevated leg reaching down the leg as far as you can. Keep your back straight and bend from the hips. Form is more important that being able to touch your toes. Hold stretch for a ten count. Repeat three times. Switch legs.

Ankle Flexibility

1. Sit in your chair and extend your leg (or cross your legs if you can). Pretend that you are writing the alphabet with your foot. Do both upper case and lower case. And try cursive! Do each foot.

Back stretch #1

1. Lower chair so knees are at a ninety-degree angle.
2. Sit facing forward.
3. Twist your upper body to the right as far as you can. Try to look behind you. If your chair has arms, grab the arms of your chair to help you twist. Hold for ten seconds switch sides, do three times.

Back stretch #2

1. Lower your desk chair so your feet are flat on the floor.
2. Lean forward, resting your upper body on your thighs. Let your hands fall naturally.

Back stretch #3

1. Clasp your hands in front of you, arms fully extended.
2. Raise your clasped hands until they are over your head. Reach up as high as you can. Count to ten and repeat three times. (If we are plus size and cannot keep your hands in clasped position when they are over your head, grasp a towel between your hands.)
3. Clasp your hands behind your back. Pull your arms down and back, puff out your chest, and bring your shoulder blades together. Hold the stretch for ten seconds. Do three times. (If you cannot reach your hands, grasp a towel between your hands.)

Upper arm/shoulders/chest

1. *Chair Pull/Push* (if your desk chair has wheels)
   a. Sit at your desk. Lift your feet. Push yourself away from your desk until your arms are fully extended.
   b. Gripping the edge of your desk, pull yourself back.
   c. Push and pull ten times.

2. *Farewell to Flabby Arms or Goodbye Angel Wings*
   a. Stand with your back to the wall, close enough to be able to touch your palms to the wall behind you.
   b. Push your palms into the wall. Hold that contraction and count to five. Repeat three times.
3. *Isometric Prayer Push*
   a. Put hands together in front of your chest in a "prayer" position
   b. Push your hands together and hold it for a count of ten.
4. Triceps Stretch
   a. Point elbow toward the ceiling, allowing your upper arm to fall behind your head.
   b. Grasp elbow with the opposite hand and gently pull elbow toward head. Hold stretch for a count of ten. Repeat with other arm.

Hands stretch

1. Extend your arm in front of you, holding your palm out as if signaling "Stop." Pull your fingers back with you opposite hand. Count to ten, repeat three times.
2. Clasp your hands in front of you. Extending your arms, raise your clasped hands until they are over your head. Stretch straight up, count to ten, repeat three times. (If you are plus size and cannot keep your hands in clasped position when they are over your head, grasp a towel between your hands continue to raise your extended arms above your head.)
3. Never leave your hand resting on your mouse for prolonged periods of time. Moving your hand often will prevent stiffness.

~ SHERRY NETHERLAND
© 2008 Sherry Netherland
www.HealthlandFitnessHumorist.com
www.FitAtAnyAgeAndAnySize.com

Whispers of Wisdom

WHISPERS OF WISDOM

*A*s women in business, we play many roles, presenting many faces to the world. However, as women, mothers, and wives in business, there is much more to us than what the world sees. Something from deep within us calls out, begging to be heard. We hear it in the middle of our workday; we see it in situations we wish would have turned out differently. We sense this presence when we witness someone else's pain; it tugs at our hearts when we look into the eyes of the children we gave birth to. Something from within our core makes us ache when we see people around the world in conflict, or nearer in our local communities; especially if it is in our own homes.

We feel this connection in life moments of great joy such as births and celebrations, and in the simple moments of joy such as inhaling the fragrance of a perfectly created rose or stroking an animal. We also feel it when we have life-altering decisions to make. What is it? What is it we feel and sense yet know not how to describe? How can something that dwells within us be unknown to us? How do we open up to our own inner sense of knowing? Is this our so-called feminine intuition—or is it something much greater?

There is a sure way to find out—sit quietly and ask those same questions again—breathe deeply, surrender completely, and listen intently. As a certified tea specialist and inspirational author, I encourage people to sit with a cup of tea and while sipping silently, to relax totally, release freely, and refresh purposefully.

Holding a cup of this steaming hot beverage opens up all of the senses—thus making it a total sensory experience—one that the body will remember—a mind, body, heart, and soul experience.

The mind is quieted, the body is relaxed, the aroma is familiar and soothing, the liquid from the infused leaves wake up the taste buds, the eyes see deeply beyond the bottom of the cup and the ears, both internal and external, tune into a new voice—an innate sound—something inherent that connects us to everything in the universe and dwells within each and every one of us. This is our heart connection to every one and every thing that is felt and heard over and over throughout our lives. This inner voice of wisdom only speaks in the language of love, for this is all it knows. Sitting with a cup of tea is one way to tune into it, and ultimately, into your real self.

Each sip is a reminder to bring the mind back to the mission of surrendering and letting go. Each breath is a release for the mind and body. Each swallow brings this magical elixir into the body in a healing and relieving manner providing rejuvenation to every cell in the body. Each moment given to this event in heart-felt surrender brings with it self-empowerment and self-fulfillment, as well as soul-empowerment and soul-fulfillment.

Each and every day in the workplace has in it the ten little minutes this ritual requires. Will you be able to shut down everything to do this for yourself? Yes, you can. Yes, you are worth it—and, no, the place isn't going to fall apart! Think about bringing a kettle to your workplace, a sentimental cup, or a tea of your choice, and claim those ten minutes of enlightenment—your co-workers, your customers, and your inner self will thank you. Then, extend this kindness to others and spread the joy around.

These precious moments with a cup of tea can also be used for moments of prayer. Delight in a few of the 101 healing prayers I have written to enjoy during tea time.

The whispering and the rustling is the awakening of your soul. The gnawing and the nudging you are noticing is the greater part of you that simply seeks to be. Put the kettle on, let everything go; breathe, open your heart, and let the journey begin. Keep smiling and keep sipping because there is always time for tea; the wisdom of the inner voice waits for thee.

~ DHARLENE FAHL-BRITTIAN
Speaker, Certified Tea Specialist, Author of Sipping Tea—Celebrating Me
www.takeupthecup.com

ACCOUNTABILI–TEA

For my actions I claim responsibility.
I hold myself lovingly in that accountability.
Every thought, word and deed has a consequence.
It is all now, there is no past tense.
God is the now, God is all there is.
We are one right now. Yesterday is gone.
Today I accept the good and become the good.
I blame no one and give
no one charge over me.
I live in divine accountability.
All I reap, I shall sow. All I think is all I know.
I know good, I do good, I am good.
In my power I proudly stand.
I walk tall with God, hand in hand;
heart to heart, soul to Spirit, One with all.
I am not alone. One for all and all for the One.
Knowing this, I live gratefully and gracefully
and I thank God faithfully.
It rarely becomes too much for me.
In the now God shows me how.
I surrender, I give in.
I let go and let God begin;
again and again.
Amen

~ DHARLENE FAHL-BRITTIAN
Speaker, Certified Tea Specialist, Author of Sipping Tea—Celebrating Me
www.takeupthecup.com

PROSPERI-TEA

Now is my time to flourish.
All the gifts of the kingdom are mine.
God knows only success,
from now on, I choose nothing less.
God is all I know. God is all there is.
Our promising, auspicious selves are one.
All outcomes are propitious and prosperous.
I thrive in the contentment of this knowledge
and this brings me infallible courage.
My every endeavour yields only good.
Because I claim all my good, all of my gifts.
Wealth and well-being go hand-in-hand;
giving is receiving, this I understand.
I accept this well-being and do well.
I give thanks and credit God, whose love
reveals my true unlimited potential.
I surrender all fears to God.
I attain and obtain all through God.
We grow and prosper as one.
I trust the Divine Wisdom, I seize the day
and God shows me the way.
Prosperity comes to me now.
Amen

~ DHARLENE FAHL-BRITTIAN
Speaker, Certified Tea Specialist, Author of Sipping Tea—Celebrating Me
www.takeupthecup.com

Responsibili-Tea

I take it easy. I keep things simple.
I break it down to what is really significant.
God matters; I matter. God is love; love matters.
I am one with God and we are all one.
Everything else that fills my life is just clutter.
I prioritize; I sort out.
I can be trusted to do a good job.
I don't have to say "yes" to everything,
but I say "yes" to the Ever-Thing,
and I say "yes" to me.
I take on the responsibility of living in accountability.
What I think, say and do, I become;
therefore, I think good thoughts, speak good words, and do good work.
I am good. I am from God—
good is all I can be.
For the divine trust put in me, I give thanks.
To those who love and believe in me,
I am grateful and faithful.
I am clutter-free; nothing blocks or hinders me.
I release having to be everything to everyone
and trust it all to the One—the forever living One,
the forever loving One.
Amen

~ DHARLENE FAHL-BRITTIAN
Speaker, Certified Tea Specialist, Author of Sipping Tea—Celebrating Me
www.takeupthecup.com

SANI-TEA

Once again, I wake up and come to my senses.
I let go and move into my divine right mind.
It is one with the One Mind, the Infinite Mind,
the mind of us all. I keep things simple,
and peace I find. God is all there is.
We are one of a kind.
This universe now responds to my mental state.
I am calm, collected and reconnected.
What I think I now set into being.
I am good, life is good, and God is good.
With the One Mind I have peace of mind.
I have a good mind and a solid mind.
Mind over matter—if I don't mind, it doesn't matter.
What I put my mind to is what appears in my life.
I give thanks and trust this Infinite Intelligence that
guides and guards me and now makes sense.
I rest my mind, I arrest my thoughts
and give my best to all that is sought.
Everything else is not up to me. I give it to God,
and I let it be. And it is all good.
What else could it be?
Amen

~ DHARLENE FAHL-BRITTIAN
Speaker, Certified Tea Specialist, Author of Sipping Tea—Celebrating Me
www.takeupthecup.com

SORORI-TEA

Honoring the divine feminine energy,
a force that unites all women,
I reconnect myself with this goddess intensity.
As sisters, we are one, one with each other,
one with God/Goddess.
A sisterhood unified by more than
a spoken vow or sacred oath.
A bond that is inseparable,
unseverable and irresolvable.
This unity strengthens our individual spirits.
It opens my heart to see my own worth and purpose,
and all that is good because all is God.
I am so grateful for the blessings of my blood sisters,
my sisters in spirit, and the Divine Presence that joins us all.
Even with the strength of a spiritual sorority,
and even in times of joy, I give it all back to God.
The solidarity of our sorority is
divinely sanctified and purified.
So I let it be and the joy of the
Sacred Feminine comes back to me.
Amen

~ DHARLENE FAHL-BRITTIAN
Speaker, Certified Tea Specialist, Author of Sipping Tea—Celebrating Me
www.takeupthecup.com

Uplifting the Spirit

The greatest achievement was at first and for a time a dream . . . Dreams are the seedlings of realities.

~ JAMES ALLEN
As a Man Thinketh

The area where we are the greatest is the area in which we inspire, encourage, and connect with another human being.

~ MAYA ANGELOU
Educator, Author, Actor, Activist, Humanitarian

It is this belief in a power larger than myself and other than myself which allows me to venture into the unknown and even the unknowable.

~ MAYA ANGELOU
Educator, Author, Actor, Activist, Humanitarian

Courage and faith go hand-in-hand. Courage is simply walking through your fear. Acknowledging it, and, with faith on your side, moving beyond fear's grip.

~ DEBBIE BARNETT
Speaker

You've achieved success in your field when you don't know whether what you're doing is work or play.

~ WARREN BEATTY

Courage is fear that has said its prayers.
~ DOROTHY BERNARD

If you can laugh at it, you can live with it.
~ ERMA BOMBECK

Faith is like radar that sees through the fog.
~ CORRIE TEN BOOM

Doubt who you will, but never yourself.
~ CHRISTINE BOVEE

Let the world know you as you are, not as you think you should be.
~ FANNY BRICE

Trust your hunches. They're usually based on facts filed away just below the conscious level.
~ DR. JOYCE BROTHERS
Psychologist and Television Personality

Your work is to discover your world and then with all your heart give yourself to it.
~ BUDDHA

A woman is like a tea bag . . . You don't know how strong she is until you put her in hot water!
~ BUMPER STICKER

The flower of a woman's wisdom blooms within her heart.
~ LAUREL BURCH
Artist Celebrating the Heart of Womankind

When your heart speaks, take good notes.
~ JUDITH CAMPBELL

Why compare yourself with others? No one in the entire world can do a better job of being you than you.
~ SUSAN CARLSON

And remember, no matter where you go, there you are.
~ CONFUCIUS

Every evening I turn my worries over to God. He's going to be up all night anyway.
~ MARY C. CROWLEY

The hardest challenge is to be your self in a world where everyone is trying to make you be somebody else.

~ E E CUMMINGS

We need to find the courage to say NO to the things and people that are not serving us if we want to rediscover ourselves and live our lives with authenticity.

~ BARBARA DE ANGELIS

Everyone needs to be valued. Everyone has the potential to give something back.

~ DIANA, PRINCESS OF WALES

It's the moment you think you can't that you realize you can.

~ CELINE DION

The minute you settle for less than you deserve, you get even less than you settled for.

~ MAUREEN DOWD

What lies behind us and what lies before us are are tiny matters compared to what lies within us.

~ RALPH WALDO EMERSON

The woman's vision is deep reaching, the man's far reaching. With the man the world is his heart, with the woman the heart is her world.
~ BETTY GRABLE

You are unique, and if that is not fulfilled, then something wonderful has been lost.
~ MARTHA GRAHAM

Our opinion of people depends less upon what we see in them, than upon what they make us see in ourselves.
~ SARAH GRAND
Novelist

Inner self-worth and self-esteem are the most important things a woman can possess . . . When our self-worth is strong, we will not accept positions of inferiority and abuse.
~ LOUISE L. HAY
Author of Empowering Women

Don't compromise yourself. You are all you've got.
~ JANIS JOPLIN

Blessed are the flexible for they shall not be bent out of shape.
~ CATH KACHUR-DESTEFANO

Life's lessons never end. A lesson is repeated until learned.
~ CATH KACHUR-DESTEFANO

Don't be afraid if things seem difficult in the beginning. That's only the initial impression. The important thing is not to retreat; you have to master yourself.
~ OLGA KORBUT
Four Time Olympic Gold Medal Gymnast

When we love and accept ourselves, we shine. To shine, we must be true to ourselves whether it be in our choice of career, expressing our truth during a conflict, or taking care of ourselves. Self-love is the foundation of any sparkle we hope to create in this world. And when we love and accept ourselves, we create sparkle for all to see.
~ ANNMARIE LARDIERI

Make your day by becoming and being the person who makes your heart smile.
~ MARIA MARSALA

Never doubt that a small group of thoughtful, committed citizens can change the world. Indeed, it's the only thing that ever has.
~ MARGARET MEAD

Men look at themselves in mirrors. Women look for themselves.
~ ELISSA MELAMED

The most important words you will ever hear are the words you say to yourself.
~ MONA M. MOON

Be willing to believe in a greater way about yourself. Let your heart be receptive to God's Spirit and guidance. Have the courage to make the decision to allow the possibility of greatness in you. Take risks beyond your boundaries, and God is right there with you.
~ MARY MANIN MORRISSEY
Author of Life Keys

I know God will not give me anything I can't handle. I just wish that He didn't trust me so much.
~ MOTHER TERESA

I am a woman above everything else.
~ JACQUELINE BOUVIER KENNEDY ONASSIS

Your Being is an unfathomable mystery of wonder and beauty. Turn your gaze inward and see what is there. Then, honor that Being.
~ PEGGY O' NEILL

Women don't listen to the voice inside them. We get our lives so busy—it [intuition] is a gift from God.

~ MARIE OSMOND

You teach people who you are by the way you treat yourself.

~ LYNN PIERCE
Author of Change One Thing, Change Your Life

When you find peace within yourself, you become the kind of person who can live at peace with others.

~ PEACE PILGRIM

I am Woman—Hear me ROAR!

~ HELEN REDDY

Self-esteem is only one of the factors that should be considered when we look to develop ourselves. Another factor is self-acceptance including loving ourselves, or at least not negatively judging ourselves, when we feel helpless, inferior and vulnerable. Self-esteem alone does not determine your ability to live your life fully. You are a unique human being. You should know what is good about you, accept your strengths and carry them with you into the world. Love who you are becoming.

~ MARCIA REYNOLDS, PsyD, MCC
Speaker, Author of Capture the Rapture: How to Step Out of Your Head and Leap Into Life

There is nothing more important or meaningful in life than honoring your authentic self—your true nature—and expressing it in the world. When you do you are allowing your Light to shine and touch the world. Living authentically, in its simplest terms, is living your Truth, in your heart and soul . . . and being real in every sense. When you are living an authentic life, you are contributing your soulful nature and gifts to the world and, thus, creating a better, more authentic and soulful life experience for us all.
~ VALERIE RICKEL
Founder and Soul, www.SoulfulLiving.com

Remember always that you have not only a right to be an individual, you have an obligation to be one. You cannot make any useful contribution in life unless you do this.
~ ELEANOR ROOSEVELT

God made man, and then He said, "I can do better than that," and made women.
~ ADELA ROGERS ST. JOHNS

Don't back down just to keep the peace. Standing up for your beliefs builds self-confidence and self-esteem.
~ OPRAH WINFREY

SHERYL ROUSH

Sparkle-Tude™ Expert Sheryl Roush presents retreats and inspirational programs that rekindle the spirit, raise the bar, and create excitement.

Humorous, creative and authentic, she relates her real-life experiences in a positive, lighthearted way that enriches the soul. She playfully engages audiences, offering valuable how-to tips while entertaining with stories, songs and surprises. Audiences "experience" her presentations—with lasting feelings, results and significance.

She was the third woman to earn the elite status of Accredited Speaker as honored by Toastmasters International (in 106 countries) for outstanding platform speaking and professionalism. Sheryl was crowned "Ms. Heart of San Diego" for 2004 and 2005, and "La Reina de Esperanza" 2007 (Queen of Hope) for contributions to the community. Sheryl was selected by Toastmasters to receive the 2009 Presidential Citation from a field of over 253,000 members.

Sheryl has presented on programs alongside Olivia Newton-John, Jane Seymour, Art Linkletter, Thurl Bailey, *Good Morning America's* Joan Lunden, *Men are from Mars* author John Gray, Howard Putnam and Geena Davis.

Have Sheryl present an energizing keynote opening—or a wrap-up sensational closing—for your event!

Highly customized workshops, special events and retreat facilitation.

Sparkle Presentations, Inc.
Sheryl@SparklePresentations.com
www.SparklePresentations.com
Call Toll Free (800) 932-0973 to schedule!

Are low morale, high-stress and poor attitudes affecting your customer service, productivity, and teamwork today?

Need to rekindle the spirit in your organization?

Bring in Sheryl Roush to energize positive trends!

Sparkle Presentations offers inspirational programs that rekindle the spirit, raise the bar, and create excitement. Programs are highly-tailored, highly-engaging, and loaded with valuable how-to's for immediate application.

Ideal for conference keynotes, retreat facilitation and in-service training: Attitude & Morale Boosters • Customer Service • Public Speaking Skills • Team Tactics • Supervisory Skills • Sales & Marketing

While at Starwood Hotels & Resorts I had the pleasure of working with Sheryl for four years, and over 150 of the managers were wowed by her training prowess, which had a major impact on the organization. We would recommend Sheryl to any other company, whether in the hospitality industry or not, as a trainer and public speaker. Sheryl's professionalism and enthusiasm are infectious! Her training has helped bring the management team of the Zoological Society to another level altogether, and we look forward to each new class she brings to our organization. I couldn't endorse her any stronger.
— Tim Mulligan, Director of Human Resources, Zoological Society of San Diego

Clients include:

7-Up
Blue Cross
California Escrow
  Association
Cal SAE
County of Los Angeles
  Management Council
Fresno County Office of
  Education
Health Care Finance
  Management Association
Hong Kong Baptist
  University

IBM—Women in
  Management
Institute of Real Estate
  Management
Latham & Watkins, LLP
Macerich Shopping Centers
Philips Morris of Asia
PIHRA and SHRM
San Diego Chargers
Sheraton
Sony
Southwest Airlines
Stampin' Up!

UCLA
Union Bank
Verizon Wireless
Women in Business
  Symposiums
Women in Publishing Society
Womens' Council of Realtors
US Census Bureau
US Olympic Training Center
Verizon Wireless
Westin
Zoological Society of San
  Diego

OTHER BOOKS AVAILABLE FROM
Sheryl Roush

Corazón de Mujer
(Heart of a Woman in Spanish)

Heart of the Holidays

Heart of the Holidays
with bonus Music CD

Heart of a Mother

Heart of a Mother
with bonus music CD

Heart of a Woman

Heart of a Military Woman

Sparkle-Tudes®:
Quotations By, For & About Women